The Passing of Pilot Officer Prune

Bill Hooper

'... permanently bone-headed, he invariably made a muck of everything he set out to do, and yet survived to make another. From the smoking wreckage of his latest 'Prunery', miraculously safe as ever, he contemplated with a hurt and puzzled detachment the incomprehensible eccentricities of a world which was never quite within his grasp; a world in which undercarriages never came down of their own accord and he never understood why.'

By the same author:
Clangers in Uniform -
  with Lt. Col R. J. Dickinson.

First published in 1975 by
MIDAS BOOKS
12 Dene Way, Speldhurst,
Tunbridge Wells, Kent.

© Bill Hooper 1975

ISBN 0 85936 025 3

Printed in England by Artographic Limited,
Haywards Heath.

FOREWORD
BY DEREK NIMMO

I really was most frightfully pleased to have my old friend, Percy Prune's, autobiography dedicated to me and also to be asked to re-introduce him to those who may not know him. His own doings during his war-time service in the Royal Air Force and his "blind stroll down Civvy Street" since the war are very much in accord with the activities of those inept characters I have done my best to portray.

As in the job of flying combat aircraft, there are pitfalls for the 'Prune-type' in Holy Orders, as I trust I've shown in "Oh Brother" and "All Gas and Gaiters", and, as a television monk and bishop's chaplain, I have some affinity with an ancestor of Percy Prune's in that he did in fact enter a monastery - or what he thought was a monastery. He was, so Bill Hooper tells me, one Paul 'Beau' Prune - 1740—1786, mentioned in this book, who, after an unfortunate love affair, entered that orgiastic 'Order of St Francis of Wycombe' - or the Hell-Fire Club - although 'Beau' never did realise what he'd got himself into and for a while he thoroughly enjoyed being a 'monk' with all those dolly-bird 'nuns' provided at Medmenham Abbey by the naughty Sir Francis. 'Beau' eventually died in Penury where he'd gone for a rest cure.

Idiotically enough, playing the fool isn't easy - to become a convincing major chump takes a lot of hard work but I think Prune has achieved it and Bill, his cartoon-creator, flatters me that I have too.

I enjoyed reading 'The Passing of Pilot Officer Prune' and I am sure that you will laugh at it as much as I did.

PAUL 'BEAU' PRUNE 1740—1786

DEDICATION

THE PASSING OF PILOT OFFICER PRUNE
Is respectfully and cheerfully dedicated to Mr Derek
Nimmo who, in the cover design, is seen holding a portrait
of Percy Prune. I have considerable pleasure in making this
dedication in gratitude to Derek for many hours of
entertainment with his 'Prune-like' humour. On stage, I
find him the perfect Prune and venture to say that had my
character, Percy, ever contemplated going into the Church
or, as he himself expressed it, "entering a monkery", after
his R.A.F. service, instead of retiring to Ineyne Manor as
Squire of Prune Parva, he'd have been as delighfully inept
as Derek's famous characters. Prune would perhaps say "I
couldn't have done better myself" which, come to think of
it, isn't saying much for Derek! I am sure that he, however,
will take all this in the spirit of admiration for his work
which I intend by this small tribute.

Bill Hooper

Introduction

Pilot Officer Percy Prune was famous in the war-time Royal Air Force, in fact he came to be as well-known as any of the aces but, whereas their renown came through achievement, Prune's notoriety was for non-achievement — or, more often, for achievement in the wrong direction and he was not so much well-known as notorious.

He was the fool, the poop, the boob, the mug, the mutt, the butt, the clot, the affable dim-wit of the RAF. Fatuously exuberant yet permanently bone-headed, he invariably made a muck of everything he set out to do. And yet survived to make another. From the smoking wreckage of his latest 'prunery', miraculously as safe as ever, he contemplated with a hurt and puzzled detachment the incomprehensible eccentricities of a world which was never quite within his grasp; a world in which undercarriages never came down of their own accord before his landings, and he never understood why — a world in which his famous finger went unerringly to the wrong 'tit'. Prune tried, but never learned. He was willing, but wet. He was dutiful but dumb. He was one in a thousand — nay a million. He can be hailed as 'one of the Few', the very few, which was as well for the Allied Air Forces and the RAF in particular.

In cartoon form Prune served throughout the hostilities as an awful warning of what not to do in an aircraft and in short order some unfortunate error of judgement could earn individual pilots the nick-name 'Prune' among their fellow flyers but then there was a little bit of him in all of us. Prune's own casual attitude toward operational flying was often the echo of real pilots' errors so that some of his cartoon adventures had sometimes been played out to a sick end in real life before his cartoon-creator, Bill Hooper, could get brush to paper. Hooper was serving on 54 Squadron, resting on a quiet field in the North of England, licking its wounds after the alarums and excursions of 1940 in the South-East. On the strength of his illustration of a book of hints and tips to fighter pilots, based on lessons learned the year before in the

6   Battle of Britain, in collaboration with his CO, Squadron Leader James 'Prof' Leathart, DFC,* called 'Forget-Me-Nots-For Fighters', he was asked by a certain Flight Lieutenant A. A. Willis at the Air Ministry to evolve a dim-wit character to carry the message to potential 'Prunes' in the pages of an official training manual to be called 'Tee Emm'.

When the RAF took 'Tee Emm' and Prune to its heart, those messages of caution, written by experts and edited by the instigator of 'Tee Emm' (later Squadron Leader A.A.Willis, O.B.E., M.C., who, as Anthony Armstrong was the celebrated playwright of 'Ten Minute Alibi', etc., etc. and as 'A.A.' was of pre-war 'Punch' fame), were sometimes taken to heart.

Some of Prune's sins and the outrageous excuses he made for them often struck home to a real-life, embarrassed, pilot's conscience but, as Prune was once heard to say, 'You can't make an omelette without spilling milk, and, if the cap fits it won't fall over deaf ears!' Not long after the war, in comfortable circumstances in Bill's cottage in Sussex, at a safe distance of time from demobilisation, ex-Flt-Lt Jimmy Edward DFC, and Bill Hooper were chatting. Bill asked Jimmy whether he still did 'any flying' and Jimmy replied with a typical 'duration bird-man's' candour and understatement, 'No, it's too bloody dangerous.' — which of course it was, but if war-time pilots and their crews could be convinced of this, at no cost to their courage, convinced through laughter at the 'other bloke's' errors — then Prune could be reckoned to have done his job.

Percy Prune, PO, had an answer for everything and was a master of what the RAF called the 'line-shoot'. Those violent ploughings-in of his aircraft, in flashes of fire and clouds of smoke and dust, which brought fire-tender and red-crossed 'blood wagons' speeding across the war-time aerodromes, were regarded by Prune as 'perfect three-point' landings — 'two wheels and a nose!'

Serving in Bomber Command, he was heard over his radio to remark to his crew during a pause in his singing of dirty songs (*and* when an overall order for radio silence was in force) 'Southend is very noisy tonight'. At that

*Air Commodore James Leathart CB, DSO, DFC, (RAF retired)

moment he was passing over the Coastal Defences of
Occupied France. On his return from a raid on
Ludwigsburg (at the briefing everybody else had
understood that the target for that night was Pfullendorf
(but Prune said that he couldn't spell that), he said the
flak was so thick that — 'just for a lark, I selected wheels
down and actually made a temporary landing on it'.

He had the normal operational pilot's disdain for 'top
brass' and on seeing a visiting Air Vice Marshal in the
mess, a gentleman whose cap was covered with
'scrambled egg' and whose left breast bore a five-decker
set of 'fruit salad', Prune said 'I'll bet he's been in the
Air Force since Pontius was a pilot'.

When he flew anything larger than a single-seater
aircraft he used up crews at an alarming rate because,
while aircraft and aircrew could be a write-off, Prune
sustained only superficial injuries. Grinning bravely, he'd
philosophise that 'A good landing, old horseman, is one
you can walk away from'. Thus Prune lived to prang
another day and some of this alarming bravado must
have brushed off on members of the crew, with which
Anthony Armstrong and Bill Hooper surrounded him. His
navigator, Flying Officer Fixe, was heard to say, in the
foetid atmosphere of a seedy RAF-type club, just off
Windmill Street, a place called the 'Ad Asbestos', 'Prune
and I came back with the entire tail-unit shot away and
we were so low over the Channel that we both had to
stand up to see over the waves'. His wireless operator,
Sergeant Backtune, was a mite casual. At a Board of
Enquiry, involving the loss of "P for Percy", a Halifax, he
said 'Well, you see Sir, nobody knew what actually hit us,
as we were all having our sandwiches at the time'.

Not everybody in the RAF was certain that in fact
Prune *was* an imaginary person — after all there was
'proof' of his existence contained in the secret, official,
telephone directory of the Air Ministry because,
dead-pan, the Editor of 'Tee Emm', Anthony Armstrong,
had told a humourless Civil Servant, who was helping to
compile the directory, that the vacant chair and desk in
his office (provided for Bill Hooper whenever he came
off-Squadron to do some cartoons) was that of 'Pilot

Officer P. Prune, Special Duties Branch' and this duly appeared in the official directory. After this a variety of people telephoned his number — including 'The Chief', Lord Arthur Tedder,* Marshal of the Royal Air Force. Usually these enquiries were answered by Squadron Leader A. A. Willis who would say that Prune was not yet back from lunch and when a certain 'Waaf Queen', who was making a list of people for a cocktail party, said that it was not yet midday, Willis countered with 'Ah, but I mean *yesterday's* lunch'.

When Bill Hooper was seconded to a Free French Squadron he was brought to realise that, like Baron Frankenstein, he had created something which was getting out of hand! In the mess at Biggin Hill a French pilot, said to have been the "unluckiest" to have flown under the Cross of Lorraine, remarked to him casually and modestly that that morning he had 'got a 'Un'. Hooper was staggered but when he mentioned it to his French Commandant, the great Commandant Rene Muchotte said 'Yes, Bill, but 'e didn't shoot 'im down, he *collided* with 'im over the Channel'. This gave Hooper the inspiration for a Gallic Prune and so 'Aspirant Praline' was born, his, Praline's, 'father', being Colonel Bernard Duperier, C de G, DFC (and a lot more).

When Prune was well-established, the Most Highly Derogatory Order of the Irremovable Finger was instituted by "A.A." and this 'decoration' was awarded each month by the Editor of 'Tee Emm' for any instance of an outstanding ability to do the wrong thing at the wrong time — while flying. Percy Prune, inevitably, was appointed the Patron of the Order and, while not pillorying individual pilots and aircrew members by mentioning names, they were 'gazetted', when their sins were reported. The Editor, no respecter of rank, instanced the boob of an Air Vice Marshal who 'visited' a certain aerodrome by air. He was saluted all over the place, and then taken to the Mess where he made a reasonable enough excuse to leave the room — in fact this was so that he could take a furtive look at the notice board to find Daily Routine Orders — and to see on this notice just what aerodrome he'd landed *on*. This 'prunery' was

* Then *Sir* Arthur Tedder

instanced in one issue of 'Tee Emm' and in the next month's issue, the irrepressible Willis published 'the letters of two Air Vice Marshals' who'd written in to say 'How did you know about me?'

'Finger!' invented by 'A.A.' and noised about squadrons and Commands by Hooper, soon became the pithy admonition to get, what the American pilots called, less subtly, 'the lead out of your arse'. It could be used, quite politely, by non-commissioned crew to pilot, with a, 'Finger — Sir!' The response was usually instant. Bill Hooper sat with a Polish pilot in a Blenheim one night, waiting to be taken off — but there was no flare path to light their way. They waited for a while and then the Polish officer said into his R/T — 'Finker' and the whole field was instantly lit up like Piccadilly.

This single-word admonition worked well when Allied pilots were covering the advance of troops against the Japanese in the 'jungle' in the final phases of the war in the Far East. The British airmen bombed and gunned what they thought to be enemy military installations but which in one case were the huts of working parties of Allied prisoners of war. To protect themselves from further raids the POWs painted 'British' on the roofs in white-wash. But, thinking that this was just another 'wily Oriental' trick, the planes went in again and gave the place another clobbering. Then a skeletal RAF prisoner climbed up, with a bucket and brush, and painted "Finger" on each roof. The strafing ceased *immediately* — the attacking pilots felt that no Jap could think up that one.

Prune came to be recognised by the United States Air Force which, later on, had its own 'Dilbert' but the distinction which the 'Yanks' accorded Percy was a doubtful one. Hooper's cartoon character was plagiarised. An inept drawing of Prune over the caption 'Be like PO Prune — and zip your lip!'' was circularised. The Americans had sadly missed the point — Prune was the last bloke to 'zip' his lip, in fact, with his back to one of those famous 'Careless Talk Costs Lives' posters, by Fougasse, he'd say, over that 'last one for the road', that he'd 'better get back to base — to make an early take-off

10   for convoy duties', and next day, limping toward the haven of Liverpool, the Merchant Navy would wonder just what had hit them.

It is therefore a little depressing, these days, to see in a recognised British reference book on slang, that, under 'Prune', the compiler explains the word as 'An American Air Force term for an inefficient pilot'.

In more recent times a popular American television series introduced an 'award' which the producers called 'The Fickle Finger of Fate' — why this was awarded and why the 'award' was given the 'Finger' — we'll never know — it was certainly as inept as 'Zip Your Lip'.

To be plagiarised is, in a way, to be complimented — and perhaps the best back-handed compliment Prune received was also, no doubt, the accolade for Willis and Hooper and it came from an unexpected quarter, from the Enemy in fact.

Shortly after hostilities had ceased, Bill Hooper received a scroll from a friend of his serving in the Captured Documents Department in Berlin. Under that ominous swastika and eagle symbol of the Third Reich and over the facsimile signature of 'Der Reichminister Der Luftfahrt Und Oberefehlshaber Der Luftwaffe — Hermann Goering' was a citation. Percy Prune had been recommended by someone in the Luftwaffe, who had a sense of humour, for the award of the Iron Cross 'for having destroyed so many Allied aircraft!'

Child Prune

Percy Prune made his first ever three-point landing on the same day of the same month in which the Royal Air Force was established — April 1st. This date may not be appropriate to the RAF as a whole, but it *was* entirely appropriate to Percy — even so, he was late.

He first saw the light o' day in the bedchamber of Lady Priscilla Prune (neé Nitte) at Ineyne Manor, Prune Parva, Sussex, where he had been expected on March 28th — according to the family doctor, his father, the nurse and Clotte, the butler. For more than forty years the butler had taken a privileged but highly inquisitive interest in the family's affairs, but Percy actually arrived four days late — but then four days on an ETA* was nothing to the Prune of later years.

Ineyne Manor is a rambling old house, perfectly matched by its rambling old butler, who, on Friday March 31st 1922, was abed in his room somewhere in the upper regions of the ancient pile having nightmares about the Boer War while Peter Prune, the expectant father, had hummed himself to sleep in his dressing room with snatches of Royal Flying Corps ballads in the worst taste. In that chamber where the historic accouchement was soon to take place, Eliza Fullboddy, the nurse, on watch, stirred in her sleep on a couch with the rumbling of a shifting avalanche.

It was 4.0 am exactly on the morning of Saturday, April 1st 1922 that the musty silence of the ancient Manor was broken by the loud and prolonged wailing of an infant. This silence was the first of many things that Prune was to break — right down to his most recent pile-up with a Jaguar on the Chiswick fly-over last August.** Child Percy was heard, not unnaturally, by all within earshot but only just by his father who was, at the time, engaged in a dream dog-fight with a pilot in Baron von Richthofen's 'Circus' over Flanders and, as Peter hazily surfaced, he was imagining that the screaming was caused by the wind through the struts and wires of his Bristol Fighter as he dived in flames to earth — which

* 'Estimated Time (of) Arrival' — over target
** Should now read Continental Juggernaut on the Portsmouth Road a week before this volume went to press.

12   indeed he had — with depressing regularity, during World War I. Only partially awake, and suffering from a chronic hang-over, occasioned by several premature drinking sessions to celebrate this overdue birth, he got the muzzy impression that in fact what he had heard was the last failing notes of the siren call to the Parva Fire Brigade, of which he was the hereditary Fire Chief.

With some confused resolve to set an example to the peasants, he pulled on his war-time flying boots and, still in his pyjamas, quit the house and trotted the half mile to the Fire Station, a shed at the back of the Mug and Finger Inn. Here he waited a while for the rest of the Brigade — George and Sid; then, in the following order, Squire Prune tried to rouse the landlord; had some empty bottles thrown at him as an intruder; tried to see if the fire-engine had already gone, then made a forced entry into the 'station'. In the lighting of several matches which he found there — to see his way around, he set light to the straw which had been put down for Old Faithless, the horse which drew the 'engine'. O.F. was an animal of a marked tetchiness of character and he kicked over a large oil drum and spilled its contents all over the floor.

This enlivened the scene considerably since the drum had contained paraffin*for the lamps of the Mug and Finger. Prune had been about to throw it over the blazing straw, believing it to be water. He ended up by burning the fire station, together with the engine, the hoses and all the equipment. He was lucky to escape with his life for Old Faithless, in a selfish bid to save his own life, panicked and knocked Squire Prune to the ground and trampled on him to get out. The landlord of 'The Mug', Bert Ullidge, not unnaturally fully awake by then, dragged his unconscious seigneur from the flaming shed and carried him into the back parlour of the pub where Prune spent the next few hours restoring himself with free brandy and taking all the credit for being the first and only member of the Parva Fire Brigade on the scene of the fire. George and Sid, the rest of the Brigade, joined him at their usual time at 'The Mug' — three quarters of an hour before opening time which, in those enlightened parts was 10 am, and the three firemen, along with

*Known to Colonials as Kerosene.

several locals who had a nose for hospitality and free drink, celebrated their landlord's safe delivery.

News of the other safe delivery, that of his son, had been conveyed by Clotte to an empty bed. The butler imagined that the strain of waiting for Percy had unhinged his master's brain and that in the small hours he had ranged out of the Manor to do himself some mischief. The unhinging of a Prune brain is too ridiculous to contemplate, even so, PC Ponder was summoned to the big house and while the Squire and his cronies were hitting it up at 'The Mug', the policeman and most of the domestics were dragging the lake and beating the coverts for his body.

Long after closing time, Squire Prune got back to a more or less deserted Manor, tumbled into his tumbled bed and, drunk as a fiddler's bitch, he slept until tea-time when another series of wails from Baby Percy almost sent him out again to the fire-station. Old Clotte, however, managed to get it through to the Squire that he now had a son. The pair of them cracked a bottle to mark the auspicious moment and Peter, having 'got the taste', went straight back again to the Mug and Finger to start in drinking all over again.

Percy Prune was not what one would call a prepossessing baby. His face was vacuous in the extreme — even for a baby's, which is saying something, and (which is saying a lot more) even for a Prune. When Clotte invited the rest of those 'below stairs' to come to Lady Priscilla's bed-chamber for the traditional first view of what Clotte called 'The new h'object', most of them gasped while the more devout crossed themselves. Unlike Percy in the aircraft cockpit in much later years, however, Baby Prune now found the right 'button', didn't press it but sucked on it and so continued to thrive.

On his return from the inn that night Squire Prune teetered to the side of his son's cot and gave the sleeping infant a long, hard stare and then he went out of the room and walked, or rather *got*, up and down the staircase several times, peering at family portraits to reassure himself, if possible, that there had indeed been *some* sort of precedence for his first-born (and, as it turned out, his last-born) in previous generations of Prunes. Peter finished up before a full-length mirror where he took another long look — this time at his own reflection. He had to admit, over that 'one for the bed' which he took in his study, that if there'd been no other before — he was, himself, a living precedent for Percy and afterwards he took steps to celebrate the event.

Squire Peter and Old Clotte searched the attics of Ineyne Manor for bunting and flags which had been hung out on similar occasions in past times and the gardener, Turnsodde, put these up — including one that the Squire thought must be 'An Eastern flag — probably Bessarabian', which, suspended over the front doors of the Manor, read ˌS∀Ǝꓘ,

Peter Prune invited all his friends and the villagers of the Parva to a series of parties and he took over the firing off of maroons and rockets, with Clotte and Turnsodde assisting, and matching him, in ineptness. The old mansion was brilliantly lit up for several nights — so was the master. At the eleventh hour on the fifth night, Peter, Turnsodde and Clotte ignited the touch-paper of a huge set-piece, which glowed with the words of the family motto, 'Semper Inanum', against the walls of the West Wing and this part of the Manor was brilliant with coloured fire, in fact by half-past eleven it was gutted.

The nursery at Ineyne Manor still bears signs of Percy's passing. The panes of all the windows which overlook the home-park are peppered with tiny holes made by mis-hits of shells from his toy howitzers when he was shooting at his toy soldiers. Half the nursery table and a window casement are charred and blackened where he overset a table-lamp while melting down his soldiers to make more shells. When he had a stock-pile of shells, however, he had no soldiers to shoot at — they had all been melted.

Percy's father, Peter 'Ropey' Prune, was born in 1889 — he died in 1925. He had served as one of the original 'Hell's Angels' in the First World War and succeeded in destroying twenty-seven aircraft — mostly Bristol Fighters and Sopwith Camels. He was invalided out of the Royal Flying Corps and given a job in the Ministry of Aircraft Disposal.

16   When Percy was three years old 'Ropey' took to the air
once more — shortly, very shortly, before he came down
again. He had been fired by the example of the intrepid
bird-men of those times — especially that of Alcock and
Brown in their epic flight across the Atlantic and he set
out on a solo trip to America. In his own aircraft he took
off from Mansden and climbed — and climbed, and then
attempted to 'straighten out' but his joystick had got
caught in the (then) new-fangled zip fasteners of his
flying-suit trousers flies. In spite of every effort to unzip
himself he continued to climb and actually achieved a
new altitude record but, having no oxygen, he blacked out
and his aircraft spiralled to earth a mere two miles from
take-off point — with fatal results — his joystick still
caught up in the zip.

Percy Prune's childhood was as tranquil as that of any
child of privilege. Only figuratively speaking was he born
with a silver spoon in his mouth but another spoon, one
which bore the arms of the Prunes, was actually left in his
mouth by Eliza Fullbody and he almost choked — Eliza
was a wet nurse, in more senses than one. He had the
usual child ailments but a good deal of the time which he
spent abed at home, or in the cottage hospital, was due to
his own ineptitude. At the age of five he overbalanced
and fell into a deep pond called Pelham's Pool while
collecting duck and swan feathers to make himself an
Indian headress. At five and a half he almost broke his
neck when he fell from a tree in the gardens. He had
spent a busy morning with 'his little axe' which, like
George Washington, he had been given as a present, and
'the axe's edge did try' and he chopped away
industriously at a high branch while sitting on the outer
end of it. At five and a half he fell out of the first floor
window and into the area of the Prune town-house, while
throwing pennies to a barrel-organist — fortunately on to
his head. During the following Christmas celebrations he
almost choked when he took a huge spoonful of
Christmas pudding and 'found' the lucky coins which
Cook had put into it. At Charing Cross Hospital, the
doctor cashed up and found that this totalled five
shillings and threepence since Cook had put in a 'lucky

three-penny bit', a 'lucky sixpence', a 'lucky florin' and even a 'lucky half-crown' — and Percy had got the lot in his dollop of pudding.

By half past five, on his sixth birthday, he was again in hospital. The six candles on his cake had been set there with pins which went into the wax and, absent-mindedly, with his hot eyes on a little blonde girl guest, he ate the spiked candles along with the silver balls and the pink icing which spelt 'Happy Birthday Dear Percy'.

An only child's existence in a large household can be a lonely one — in later days Percy said 'A good deal of the time when Angela wasn't there I was forced to play with myself' (actually he meant play *by* himself).

The servants at Ineyne did their best to make Percy's life as pleasant as possible. Apart from Clotte, there was the footman Ernyer, who was flat-footed and walked with a peculiar straddled gait, the Cook Iris, whose surname was Tewe, two maids Rene and Queenie — (one was a 'tweeny'), Turnsodde the gardener, (and the "Virgin" of Prune Parva Church) and his son Lionel, who acted as 'boots', under-gardener and general handy-boy.

In Prune's childhood there was no electricity laid on at the Manor. The house was illuminated throughout with oil lamps — about seventy of them. It was Lionel Turnsodde's job to clean, trim and replenish these each day and young Percy used to 'help' Lionel in the 'lamp room' just off the kitchen. It was Lionel Turnsodde, a lad of eighteen, who first revealed what Percy thought to be the nicknames of the two maids. Queenie and Rene would come to the lamp room to collect the lamps to put them all over the house. Whenever young Lionel heard them approaching — with girlish chatter and giggles, he'd say 'Here comes the 'grumble and grunt'! Percy was puzzled because Rene didn't grumble and Queenie didn't grunt but the odd reference stuck in his memory and in later years — when down from Cambridge, entertaining friends at the manor, the two maids brought in sandwiches and Percy, emulating Lionel, said 'Ah! — here comes "grumble and grunt" ' — and the two maids gave in their notice next day.

The oil-lamps were filled with a mixture of colza and

paraffin which was kept in the garage. On the morning of young Turnsodde's birthday, Percy decided to fill the lamps for him. He went down while it was still dark and worked for two hours cleaning the lamps and filling them from cans in the coach-house and left them, gleaming and full, as a surprise for Lionel. Surprise it was. As the family sat down to tea late that afternoon, at a time when Lionel lit the lamps for the maids to place around the house, there was a loud explosion heard from the basement and, Clotte swore afterwards, young Turnsodde came flying backwards out of his lamp-room and into the kitchen with his bushy hair alight, resembling nothing so much as a fiery meteor. It was fortunate that the first lamp he'd lighted was some way from the rest for Percy had inadvertently filled them all with petrol.

Life brightened up a lot for Percy when his grandmother, Lady Nitte, came to live at Ineyne Manor. She used to play soldiers with him. In her girlhood, before she met Lord Nitte, Lady Naome had been engaged to a young man in the Royal Horse Guards but they quarrelled and, the gossips had it, Lord Nitte caught her on the rebound. As unkind as this may sound it was, nevertheless, quite true for their romance began when Lady Naome rebounded off a pillar at the Trocadero and Nitte caught her after the Horse Guards officer, an oafish young baronet, had struck her between the entreé and the joint. Lady Naome, however, never really got over that first romance — in fact she never truly recovered from the Blues officer's clout for her left eye had a tendency to turn inward and, as she grew progressively older after the death of Lord Nitte, she took to wearing a Horse Guards breastplate and a helmet with a red plume, at meal-times. Young Percy was intrigued by this and he and his grannie had many a jolly game of soldiers until the tragic day when her Ladyship decided to add a sword to her military get-up and this got caught between her legs on the top of the grand staircase one evening as she was coming down to dinner and she fell and broke her neck.

Even before Percy went to boarding school he had a notable 'score' of write-offs behind him. He had a cot, two cradles, a rocking-horse, two tricycles and a

junior-model bicycle to his 'credit'. His first real bike was a Christmas present, a sleek and shiny Rover. It was perhaps unfortunate that the Prunes were spending that Christmas in Town because space to learn to ride was more limited than it would have been back at Prune Parva — and Percy required all the space he could get, in fact, at a much later time, as he was mindlessly dicing in a two-seater aircraft with a steel-nerved Flying Instructor, that patient officer asked acidly whether he would "like a little more sky?"

A favourite training ground for young cyclists in central London was, in Percy's day, a then-quiet road which runs north of the Serpentine. Lady Priscilla told off Ernyer, the flat-footed footman, to accompany Master Percy and put him through his initial paces. Due to a distressing condition of the crotch (caused, Ernyer always said, through hauling a dead drunk Peter Prune out of the Ha-Ha during the Christmas celebrations of 1920). Ern' was no five-day man but he was at least able to support the boy while Percy mastered the balance and practised slow pedalling. After a week of this, when Master Percy appeared to have achieved his balance and could pedal, Ernyer took the opportunity of going off to the nearest pub, as quickly as his indisposition would allow, for a refreshing pint.

Percy had indeed mastered the balancing and could also pedal but he had not yet learned to steer and he careened off that road which runs north of the Serpentine — southward and *into* the Serpentine where he almost drowned. Ernyer, who was no running footman, threatened to give in his notice if he was ordered to go out with Percy again and so a few days later the boy sneaked out of the house to explore London on his own. He actually got as far as the Thames Embankment without serious mishap and was cycling toward Blackfriars, on the wrong side of the road, when his wheels became firmly fixed in the tram lines but he continued to cycle on, hoping that he would reach a set of points where he might wrench the wheels free. His plan was foiled by a tram, going in the opposite direction — to

Streatham in fact, and the sleek, shiny Rover was a
write-off.

Percy had had a whole parade of governesses but each had given up the job as hopeless and so he would, in the ordinary way, have been ill-prepared for placing at his boarding school — however, this school was his father's old school, St Finga's, Herts, and, by endowing a new laboratory, Lady Priscilla persuaded the governors to have Percy entered.

He actually passed the entrance exam which, in view of the crippling fees at St Finga's, was made ridiculously easy and consisted of a single question — 'Who was the father of Abraham's sons?'. After a lot of coaching beforehand and some prompting by the Proctor, Percy passed and was placed. Boys were usually entered at any age between eight and ten years — Percy tooled in at fourteen. This ancient seat of learning was described in a seventeenth century charter as 'an academie for ye fonnes of fimple gentlemenne'. Few of the pupils' fathers could have been as 'fimple' as the late Peter Prune, but at least he had been a gentleman and so there's still an obvious twist on that description.

As a fag — a 'new bug', Percy joined his schoolfellows to hare down to the dining hall with copies of 'St Finga's School Songs', during his first month, for the monthly House Singing. In the hall they all sat down on hard benches to sing the school songs while the Music Master was present to judge their individual talents by asking each new boy to give a solo performance of 'The Ash Grove'. Percy Prune attended only one of these sing-songs because after the boy who was playing the piano had gone twice over the tune — Percy recognised it as one which Lionel Turnsodde used to sing in the lamp-room at home and he gave out, with all the characteristic discordancy of the Prune voices, — "I chased her, I caught her, I gave her a baby daughter . . ." etcetera, and was hastily stifled, dragged off by a senior and thrashed. He got six hard strokes for obscenity and twelve for discordancy.

His career as a fag left a grim trail of burnt toast, scorched trousers, (which he'd tried to press) scorched mantelpieces, where he'd held newspapers to the coals to draw up the fire, and then had the paper flare up or itself be drawn up flaring into a chimney, which also caught fire, scorched sausages and a scalded back. The latter disaster occurred when a 'three yearer' told him off to run a bath but when the senior got into it he said that it was too cold and so Prune topped up the bath from a huge black kettle full of boiling water — while the fag-master was still in it.

His mother sent him a brown trilby hat to wear when he came home for his first holiday. Unfortunately when he was packing Percy sent this off with the rest of his luggage and so had to go home in his school straw hat. As with all his schoolfellows, he was the target for the derision of the 'Town boys' who, on seeing a St Fingarian in his 'straw-yard', would yell out "Who stole the donkey's dinner? STRAWYARD!" but Percy Prune was probably the only boy who actually provided a donkey with such a dinner. As he waited outside the railway station for the car which would take him to Prune Parva, he was engrossed in a copy of 'The Magnet' and a donkey, harnessed in a carrier's cart, actually ate his hat without Percy being aware of it.

A visitor to Prune Parva during this holiday of Percy's was touched by the sight of the fatherless youth loitering around the place and offered to take Percy under his wing. This good-hearted gentleman, was a certain Major "Dizz" Astor, who had served with Percy's father in the Royal Flying Corp, and he set out to tutor Percy in field sports. Percy was, however, as inept at field sports as he was at anything else and while he could "walk up" partridges well enough, with the cartridges which he fired off as a result, he knocked down one of Major "Dizz's" dogs and a keeper as well. The Major took him duck-hunting but he fired both barrels into the boards of their punt, while reloading, and sank them both in six feet of water. "Dizz" thought Percy may do less damage if he took him sea-fishing and they drove down to West Bay, Bridport, where the Major hired a small sailing boat. In this little craft, Percy flailed about him with his rod, the line of which he'd fitted with lead weights, swivels and spinner for mackerel but the Major, an experienced

sea-angler, said that there were no mackerel about
"Though", he said encouragingly, "we may get a gurnet swimming high". In fact, by an extraordinary fluke, Percy actually hooked a *gannet* flying low and in the resultant struggle with the frantic bird in the little boat, the·craft was overset and Percy and the Major had to be rescued by the crew of a pleasure boat as they clung to its keel. After this "Dizz" felt that there was a limit to what a man can do in the name of old comradeship and he put Percy on a train in Bridport saying that he had to cut short his holiday to attend to some estate business in London.

Back at St Finga's it was really time for Percy to move up from Middle to Upper School — in fact it was long past that time. When boys were thus elevated they cast off their juniors' Eton jacket to wear the tail-coat of maturer fellows and left off their deep Eton collars to wear an 'up and a downer' — the kind worn with full evening dress. At the age of fifteen Prune felt out of place in his Eton jacket and collar and he once said that he'd felt "grotesque" — he *looked* grotesque. The front of his 'bum-freezer' jacket barely covered his rib-cage, the cuffs were up to his elbows and he was towering above his fellow pupils. By working very hard at the intensive cribbing of brighter boys' notes and exam papers, however, he finally got changed *into* the tails of a 'two yearer' and, in the matter of a fancy waistcoat, which was allowed on Sundays, he affected a lurid confection of two inch wide Regency stripes coloured in 'egg, green and egg', — some of the 'egg' being real egg for he was a rather sloppy eater at this time.

He aspired to be an oarsman and was allowed by a heavily-tipped boatman to take out a sculler alongside another and more experienced boy. While still holding on to the pontoon, however, he fumbled his oars and stove in the other boy's sculler with one then stove in the boy's skull with the other. He then capsized his own boat and it was an hour before enough boards could be removed from the landing stage to draw him through to safety. The other boy, a real 'Wet Bob' of the school, was taken to hospital while Prune, by now a real 'Wet Perc', was firmly told never to set foot near the boathouse again.

Most of Percy's troubles at school were of his own making — as in the case of the 'Ventriloquist Set'. In a boys' magazine he chanced upon an intriguing offer, to teach people to throw their voices, and he straightway sent off the coupon and a postal order for a course of lessons and a dummy. The dummy was a disappointing sort of puppet but Prune was not discouraged. Every evening he skipped prep' to go down behind the cricket pavilion to practise and within three weeks he convinced himself that he was actually making his voice come from behind trees and the playing field fence. When he felt that he'd mastered the art, he decided to startle his Form by displaying his skill during a lesson. His English Master, Dr Bernard Busby, known to his pupils as 'Bustle Bum', had set the Form to writing and Prune, head down to his work, apparently, suddenly cried "I'm behind the blackboard Berny Busby! Come and get me Bustle Bum!" — all this without moving his lips.

None but the best of ventriloquists can master that awkward letter 'b' and so what Prune had intended to cry out actually came out as "I'ne gehind the glackgoard Gerny Gusgy! Cun and get ne Gustle Gun!" and anyway, to Busby, the voice had not come from 'gehind the glackgoard' but from Prune so Bustle Bum went straight for *him* and, since punishment in Percy's day frequently took a purely punitive form, the master simply drew off and fetched Percy a flat-handed clout which put him into the aisle.

Percy had hoped to do his voice-throwing act for the School Review at Christmas time but this initial failure discouraged him — even so, when the curtain went up on the first act of the show, there he was with another boy in the centre of the stage. The scene was that of a Transylvanian village — the setting for a short play called 'Dracula's Revenge', a piece written by a morbid-minded boy who had written it to involve blood-sucking vampires and several bottles of tomato ketchup 'blood'. Prune had been given a very small part when another boy had gone down with flu'. He was dressed as a peasant and he and

the other actor affected to listen to the strains of a violin off-stage then "First Peasant" had to say "Hark, friend, is that a Gypsy?" and Percy then gave out with his only line — which of course he mucked — "No," he quoth brightly, "'tis a piddling pheasant!"

This got the show off to a good start and later, as one of Robin Hood's Merry Men in another piece, he accidentally let fly with an arrow which pinned Matron's bloomers to her bottom as she bent over in the wings. This play ended with all the Merry Men dancing round the Maypole but Prune naturally got his ribbons mixed, stopped to untangle them, and was caught like a fly in a spider's web and almost throttled by his school-mates.

Percy's only distinction at school was that he reigned for several years as 'Conker Champion'. 'Conkers' (— or, more correctly, 'Conquerors',) was one of those periodical crazes which swept schools of that time — cigarette cards, spinning tops and marbles were some others. Percy here displayed that artful inventiveness which had got a lot of past Prunes out of trouble and it was to serve him well in later life. He obtained a small cube of mahogany which industriously, and secretly, he carved into the semblance of a horse-chesnut during Handicraft Classes. He polished this tough wooden 'conker', bored a hole in it and then threaded it on to a length of string. When challenged by other boys, with real horse-chesnuts, he smashed all comers and was only discovered, just before he left school, when he inadvertently mis-hit and smashed his opponent's wrist instead of his 'conker'.

In due course — or rather after a much more extended course than any of his contemporaries, or, for that matter, generations of St Fingarians before him, Percy went up to Cambridge where he was elected to St Clewelesse College.

His mother threw a restrained little hen party when, a week later, he telephoned to tell her that he'd got "an Exhibition!" What Prune's Cambridge Tutor had actually said, rather testily, was that he was "an exhibitionist" but this was not altogether Percy's fault because he'd got in with a doggy crowd of fellows who were themselves so dim that they hardly noticed Percy's clottishness — in fact they thought him "no end of a fellow" and of course he played up to them. His coterie preferred heavy drinking to deep study and, gaining an unenviable reputation as grog-blossoms, they came to be known around Cambridge as 'The Peasoupers' because they were forever arranging wine, spirit and beer drinking sessions which they called "pea-sups".

Percy Prune was 'up' for just two terms — the first he spent almost permanently intoxicated. Even when sober he was thought by the Faculty to be half-cut because of his normal bemused expression and demeanour. The second term was marred by an extended stay in the Infirmary where he underwent a long course of massage for a neck injury. This was caused by his affecting a silly undergraduate fashion of his day which was in slavish imitation of members of the rowing club — the wearing of very long scarves. These went twice around the neck and still reached down to the shins and, by the more flamboyant types, were even worn with dress clothes. Percy, never one to do things by halves, had his mother and his old nurse knit him a scarf which was fully fifteen feet long, in his St Clewelesse colours. He was able to take this ridiculous scarf twice round his neck and still have it trail on the ground behind him. He also affected a huge briar pipe, which, although it caused his jaws to ache abominably, he kept firmly clamped in his mouth all the time.

One night he made a noisy departure from the Baron of Beef to go to a late-night dance. Dressed in tails, his silly scarf around his neck and large pipe stuck in his face, he gaily lurched toward Magdalene Bridge where he'd parked his Lagonda by the boat house, and dropped into the driving seat. He ran up the engine with a lot of unnecessary noise as he flung the ends of his scarf behind him and then emulated Isadora Duncan's fatal move for, as he "gave her the gun" and roared off in a tight turn and a shower of gravel, the end of his absurd neckwear caught in the spokes of a rear wheel. He was whipped, like an unwary trout, out of the driving seat, while his car veered towards the bridge. Percy was flung, to the limit of his scarf, eyes bulging and the stem of his huge pipe jammed down his throat so that only the big bowl was showing, his face puce, the veins on his forehead resembling nothing so much as spaghetti in tomato sauce, after his car.

His Lagonda hit the parapet of the little bridge, stood for an instant on its bonnet, then slowly turned right over and landed upside down in the river below while Percy, in his turn, was seen to describe a graceful arc at the end of the scarf and then he also went over, to land, with a thwack, on the cam, his head turned almost back to front.

War was declared while Percy was still in hospital and on his coming out of dock his witless cronies 'The Peasoupers', gave him a party but his resistance to strong drink had been impaired by his long period of unserviceability and he got excessively drunk. Outside the Hat and Feathers he punched a don on the nose (Percy was wearing a hat with feathers, at the time,) and for this offence, along with others, such as breaking into College (often the wrong ones, like Newnham or Girton), in a drunk and disorderly state, in the small hours, he was sent down. At home he got his call-up papers. Thus Prune had hardly gone 'up' than he was sent 'down' and was almost immediately called 'up'.

There is a regrettable lack of documentation bearing on this period in Percy Prune's life — his septic youth, other than a lot of newspaper cuttings about court cases for driving offences or being drunk and disorderly in the Cambridge and Parva areas, along with two affiliation orders issued against him at this time — all pasted with care, by a devoted mother, in 'Ye Logge Booke' of the Prunes but we did discover a photograph of Percy taken from a pre-war copy of 'The Tittler'. He is seen at the last Royal Garden Party before the outbreak of war. His cousin, 'Pongo' Prune, who was then in the Brigade of Guards, got him this invitation which led to Percy having a brief word with the King — actually he had a brief, a very brief word, *from* the King because when His Majesty remarked to Prune, apropos the situation in Europe, that this may well be "the last Royal Garden Party for a while", Percy said that, for his part, the only Royal occasion that *he* was really looking forward to seeing was a coronation! It was at this point that the Monarch said that brief word.

It is perhaps worth mentioning that 'Pongo' Prune was that same guardee who, as officer i/c the Bank of England guard, marched his guardsmen through the City of London one evening, or almost through it, wearing his bearskin so far forward over his eyes that he couldn't see where he was going and actually led them down the steps of an Underground station where he perished on the live rail just before the train for Cockfosters came in.

It was as well that Percy's call-up came only a short time after he'd been sent down from Cambridge because, having left the University in such bad odour, he was soon being asked by his mother to leave the Manor, at least for a while. He was existing there under a 10/10ths cloud for having been discovered assailing young Angela Fullboddy, the daughter of Eliza, his nurse. Eliza was a spinster with well-defined attitudes towards what she called "Nonsense". As Percy told it in later times, he and "Little Angela" who, before her fifteenth birthday, was being called *"Big* Angela", had spent their school holidays around Ineyne Manor and were always together "in the woods, in the shrubbery, the cupola, the boat-house or up in the attics, exploring all the hidden parts and ways together". These puerile pleasures, took a more serious turn when Master Percy came down from Cambridge, though by that time he had already passed through his first youthful flush of naughty thoughts and pimples. Eliza felt that there was something amiss when, as she was collecting some repaired linen from the sewing room, she heard the unmistakable cackling of Clotte, coming from the gloom of the 'Long Passage'. She went to investigate and saw Clotte on his knees looking through the key-hole of what should have been an untenanted room — the Nursery, and saying "Cor —" and "Coo!" and cackling.

Eliza briskly dismissed the butler by hitting him with a back-hander in the left ear and, entering the Nursery, found Master Percy with her daughter in the most compromising circumstances.

During the embarrassing interview with his mother

which followed this shocking discovery, Percy tried to assert himself as the Master of Ineyne — his father, after all, having passed away in 1925. Percy maintained that he had only been exercising his "doigt de seigneur" but Lady Priscilla, entirely missing the error in his French, said that *that* privilege of the squirearchy "went out long ago" and so it was a relief to everybody when Percy left to go into the RAF.

INEYNE

PETER 'ROPEY' PRUNE ESQ (EX-2nd LIEUTENANT R.F.C.) MASTER OF INEYNE 1903-1925

LADY PRISCILLA PRUNE, née NITTE

LADY NITTE

MR CLOTTE THE BUTLER

MISS ELIZA FULLBODDY, NURSE~ COOK

ERNYER~ FOOTMAN

LIONEL TURNSODDE ODD-JOB BOY

QUEENIE AND RENE

BILL HOOPER

Pilot Officer Percy Prune

RAF

Distance can lend enchantment and that's as good a reason as any for recalling the memory of Percy Prune with affection. At this distance of time it is natural enough for us to reflect upon the good fortune which brought us through the war so that we can now look back on those years of hazard to find that, in the main, the lighter side of the life we led prevails over the grimmer aspects. The normal hazards of war-time flying were always increased alarmingly for anyone who came within the erratic orbit of Prune so that those of us who survived our service from 1939 onward can count ourselves doubly fortunate that we did not become involved in the destructive and unpredictable "circuits and bumps" of Prune's own war.

Nobody can account for Prune being commissioned — for that matter his survival of basic training "on the square" at Padgate and his passing through and passing out of flying training is altogether inexplicable. The most likely explanation is that he was frequently confused in his cadet days with a certain Percy Pryne, whom he met on the Pullman coach — of the train which was taking them both to report at Padgate. Purely on the strength of the coincidence of their names and the strength of the whiskey then served on Great Western Railway trains, they both got drunk en route and were lustily singing "Here's to the next man to die", before they'd even been accepted into the RAF as air-crew-under-training.

When they did take the oath and receive their numbers, Prune was standing next to Pryne so that while Percy Prune drew 977950, Pryne was 977949. Percy stood next to Pryne when they were issued their knives, forks, spoons, mugs and shaving brushes, he stood next to him in the ranks while a patient Drill Instructor tried to teach

them (a) how to march and (b) how to do so while
carrying a rifle but, what is much more significant, Prune
sat next to Pryne, Percy, during all the lectures and tests
which followed and even slept in the bed next to Pryne's
with the latter's lecture notes and 'home-work', a bare
eighteen inches from his face, in the locker by his
namesake's bunk. In due time, while Percy Prune went to
keep an appointment at what was then Adastral House,
Kingsway, Prynne, Percy, "failed", puzzled and hurt, was
on his way to a posting and remustering from 'Air Crew
U/T' to "Clerk, General Duties".

If Prune's becoming an officer is difficult to
understand, the fact that he served in the same rank for
five years and when he was demobbed had had no
promotion whatsoever, is entirely understandable.*

Some people have been content to explain away his
commission as a clerical error while others, less generous,
say that he got into the Board Room while the 'Board'
was at lunch at Bush House and had "stamped his own
cards".

"Battle Fatigue" was an unknown phrase back in 1940
(we learned it from the Americans later on,) but it *is*
known that at least one of Prune's flying instructors went
out of the service with something like it. During initial
training after a flight, Percy complained to an Instructor
for whom he'd bought a large brandy (which was the least
he could have done for the poor fellow) that "When we
went down my ears felt funny". The veteran birdman
explained that this odd numbness was caused by
centrifugal force and to relieve the pressure on his ears —
he should shout or sing loudly. Percy mulled this over for
a while and then came back to the instructor and asked
— "What should I shout or sing?"

When, for some reason, an aircraft's undercarriage
failed to come down before landing, a warning klaxon
horn would sound in the plane. This happened when
Prune was landing with his Instructor and, turning to this
patient fellow as they walked toward the flight hut, he
said "Do you always have to sound your hooter when
coming down through low cloud?"

It is essential for an aircraft such as that which Prune

---

*A wit once suggested that he couldn't even have been 'moved up one',
to Flying Officer — "F.O." meant "Finger Out".

was given to fly solo to take off upwind and land upwind — that is why the aerodrome from which he flew first had one of those odd wind socks which indicated the wind's direction, but Prune had never really absorbed this, nor the fact that the wind direction can change so that when he was about to take off one morning, and it was pointed out to him that he was doing so down-wind, he said "That's silly — I've been taking off toward that church steeple for the past three days".

It was fatuous responses like this which put grey hairs above his instructors' ears but the white ones got there when he acted out such statements as "I can fly through any balloon barrage. I simply bank over vertically and fly through on my wing tip".

He once took over the controls in a twin-seater which his instructor ordered him to land. He came down cross-wind and barely missed a petrol bowser and the hangar and then, as he went into a climb, which was so sudden as to result in an almost perfect loop, he called out, apropos the scuttling away from his path of the ground crew, "I'll bet half the bods down there nearly messed themselves," whereupon his instructor, an honest man, said "Half the bods up here *did*".

Before Percy went to an operational squadron he was detailed to take up a trainer aircraft, Number 80. He ambled across the field and climbed into Number 60 and then carried out an assiduous cockpit check and started it up. The aircraft fired for a few revolutions but Percy felt that he should report to the Control Tower that his engine was "running very roughly". He was tersely informed that this was not altogether surprising since he was sitting in and running up an unserviceable aircraft — unserviceable, that is, in that it didn't have a propeller!

While flying an Anson trainer his radio failed and so he grabbed a Verey pistol from its housing in the cockpit, loaded it with a red cartridge to fire it with the object of giving some sort of warning to the ground personnel that he was in trouble, then thrust it back into its holder with some confused notion that this was the shute through which Verey cartridges were fired — it wasn't. The housing had no outlet to the outside of the plane and so when Percy pulled the trigger it caused a fearful red explosion (he had at least selected the right cartridge — otherwise it'd have been a green explosion) — Percy was blown out of his seat and managed to scramble out of the aircraft to bale out as the Anson went down in flames. It was as a result of this that he made history among the trainees as the first to come down by parachute. He further distinguished himself after reading an article, written by someone in the Air Ministry, about saving aircraft fuel. He took up an aircraft on an unauthorised flight, ran out of fuel and came down on the sea. It was here that he failed to take his finger out — quite literally, for although his dinghy functioned well and Prune was content enough to bob around in the Channel in his 'yellow doughnut', the little rubber boat had sprung a small leak and so Percy searched around for the leak stopper which he had heard about during lectures on 'ditching at sea'. The one he found was too big for the leak and so, without investigating further, he flung the thing away and simply stuck his finger in the hole. One by one his fingers became numb with cold and he had to change fingers frequently. He was down to the ring finger of his left hand when a craft of Air Sea Rescue came cleaving through the waves to save him. The Warrant Officer in charge told Percy that varying sizes of leak stopping plugs were always contained in the biggest one — the one he'd thrown away.

At the court of Enquiry which followed all this, when Percy was asked why he'd taken up the aircraft without permission in the first place, he referred to the Air Ministry publication about saving fuel and his defence was that he'd taken the aircraft off to "dice about for a couple of hours to practise saving fuel".

He had the devil's own luck. Before he was posted to a squadron he taxied an aircraft out at a furious rate, went off the runway, careered across the edge of the field through several bushes and then went right through a farm gate set at the limits of the aerodrome and here he stopped. The aircraft was quite undamaged, except for a few scratches from the bushes, because as he careered through the gate with everyone watching him and holding breath, the aircraft wings cleared the rest of the thick hedge., The gate, a large five-barred affair, had been left wide open and so his propeller blades and undercarriage also remained intact.

AIRBORNE

By the time he was posted to his first operational squadron Percy had already achieved an imposing 'score' of destroyed or damaged aircraft. To his 'credit' he had two Tiger Moths, an Anson and a Miles Magister. The last had not been airborne — it was just 'ticking over' on the tarmac — and Prune wasn't even sitting in it. He simply "walked into the prop" and the famous Prune skull did the rest.

In that lovely summer of 1940 we engaged the enemy at a stage of the war which the historians have set cosily between two dates — July 10th — to October 31st. It was a time of long periods of inactivity interrupted by short periods of intense activity — the Battle of Britain.

The home-station of Percy's squadron was RAF Prangmere, Sussex and the day before he arrived the field had been severely done over by the Luftwaffe in a succession of bombing raids and, only half awake, a tired flight-leader ordered the new pilot up on a weather test, advised him to get in some 'circuits and bumps' and generally render himself familiar with the surrounds of the aerodrome. Percy taxied a Spitfire out of its dispersal bay and along the perimeter track where, across his path, he encountered a line of oil drums on which several planks had been set. "Not wishing", as he said afterwards at the Court of Enquiry, "to worry Flying Control" (or even to question the reason for this obstruction) he hailed two jaded Aircraftsmen 1st Class who, with mug, knife, fork and spoon at 'the trail', were trudging across the field in the smoky dawn to get their breakfast after tuning up their aircraft on "early turn". They were singing a breezy squadron marching song to keep themselves awake until they'd got their bangers and bacon — "Early turn's a bastard and the dawn patrol's a farce, you can stick the whole of this Command right up

your f—" when they heard Prune calling to them.

Percy told the 'erks' to remove the planks and barrels which they did, after some brief but respectful argument, and then they stood by, fascinated, while Prune taxied on and down into a large bomb-crater which the oildrums and planks had been put out to mark — then the airmen went on to the cook-house.

Prune's CO took him off operational flying before he'd really got on to it and told him to "get some flying hours in" but he ripped through some telegraph wires while, as he said afterwards, "rounding up some sheep on the Downs", and then put his aircraft neatly on the roof of an earth closet in the backyard of an irate Sussex shepherd. The shepherd was irate because, on this peaceful Sunday morning, when the only sound to disturb the quiet was that of a German aircraft machine-gunning a train on the Hastings line, his father had been inside the kiosk and was, what "Prisoner's Friend" (a peace-time barrister) said later, "disarranged at his morning's dismissing". This disarrangement included having his bare-legs scorched with sparks from his pipe and his crotch scalded with hot tea, a large mug of which he'd taken into the lavatory — along with his Sunday Pictorial.

It must be said for Prune that he was never lost for an excuse and on this occasion he said, quite reasonably, he thought, that he'd had "to fly fairly low to avoid strong winds at a higher altitude".

GROUNDED

Although he was now grounded pending the Enquiry — and did nothing but hang about the airfield, he still got into trouble and was again responsible for damage to an aircraft which he wasn't flying. He was loitering about 'Works Flight', playing 'double or quits' with an Armourer Corporal when a 'Maggy' was trundled out of the hangar after a overhaul and re-doping. A mechanic climbed in to tune up the aircraft and Prune wandered over to ask whether he could sit in the cockpit and do it for him. The ground-staff saw no objection to this as long as he didn't attempt to move the aeroplane. Prune revved it up for a while and then espied a dog behind the Miles Magister. This was the Squadron Mascot, a large, tough, pink and white bull-terrier called 'Willy', which, replete on treble rations obtained at the back doors of the Officers', the Sergeants' and Airmens' Messes, ('Willy' was no snob) was a familiar sight around the aerodrome which he perambulated, keeping stray dogs off the field, with an ambling gait reminiscent of an Able-Bodied Stoker coming off the docks on shore-leave. 'Willy' was presenting the rear view of himself to Prune — an aspect which left no doubt whatsoever about his sex, when Prune "shoved her through the gate" — gave the engine full boost and raised a thick cloud of dust and a very powerful slip-stream behind the aircraft. Short of a bull-dozer, there are few things that'll shift a bull-terrier, but 'Willy' was in a vunerable pose at the time. He was poised, slightly forward, and 'pointing' out-field at a scruffy stray with which he'd had several brushes because the stray dog wanted to get in on this Squadron Mascot racket with the free vittles that went with it.

'Willy' was on the point of charging when the slip-stream caught him in the rear and pitched him, base over apex, and put him out of his boxing. Prune thought this very funny but as the slip-stream died down, 'Willy' whirled around and charged the aircraft. *Nothing* like this had happened to him before — he was a privileged animal and a full 'Group Captain' "on the strength of RAF Prangmere". 'Willy' reared up at the tail-unit of the 'Maggie' and proceeded, in a terrible silence, to rip all the fabric off it.

Prune's Commanding Officer, faced with a shortage of pilots as well as aircraft, was nevertheless determined not to risk either those aircraft — or his pilots, by having Prune in the air and he told him vaguely to "go and help the Adjutant" and when Prune asked "Help the Adjutant what?" — the CO was not at all vague in his answer and he told Prune to go and do something which is anatomically impossible.

The Adj', known to the flying personnel as 'Auntie', was a mild-mannered gentleman, a be-ribboned veteran of the First War and he put Prune to drafting out "Daily Routine Orders, Station Prangmere, RAF", for typing. Prune boobed — even in this simple job. Perhaps the first of the clangers he dropped in print was innocent enough — it appeared under the heading "Church Parades" and gave the times for the various denominations to parade — or rather it should have been under the heading of "Church Parades" but Prune struck an original note and had it as "God Bothering". At the bottom of the list of times, in writing that "Jewish and other denoms (denominations) will parade by arrangement with their individual padres", he transposed an 'n' and an 'm' so that it read "Jewish and other demons . . ." and a furious Wing-Commander-Flying, who *was* Jewish, raised Cain with 'Auntie' and accused him of being anti-Semetic.

Prune's second clerical error was more serious. The Adj' asked asked him to include a mention in D.R.Os of a shortage of clothing in the 'other ranks' ' stores and the fact that male personnel should have priority. The result appeared under the heading — "Clothing Issue" and ran — "Waafs will hold up their own clothing until the wants of the RAF are satisfied". A livid 'Waaf Queen' stormed into the Adjutant's office over the hangar — deeply concerned with the image of her service, and went so far as to smack 'Auntie's' face, Prune wasn't present — quite coincidentally, he'd put in for a forty-eight hour pass which he spent getting free drinks from grateful Cockneys in return for telling them how many German bombers he'd shot down.

If there was one accomplishment Prune possessed it was his ability to shoot a line and some of his outrageous boasts have become legend. He was asked by another pilot why he preferred one particular type of aircraft to another and Percy gave as his reason that when he was engaged in low-level strafing he always preferred the aircraft in question because its propeller blades were three inches shorter than those of the other aircraft and this enabled him to fly lower.

A harmless affectation of fighter pilots was to leave undone the top button of their tunic — in no other way could they be distinguished from what they called "bus

drivers" — the bomber pilots. Percy found himself in a
group of bomber pilots on leave in London and was
chaffed by them about this but he was in no way put out.
He said that he didn't fasten the top button of his tunic
simply because he hadn't one at that moment — it had
been shot off some twenty hours before 'in a dog fight
over the Channel'.

During his term of office as a 'caged bird' at the Air
Ministry he frequently went to enjoy a wet luncheon at
the long bar of the old Holborn Hotel, which once stood
at the top end of Kingsway, and here he was heard saying
how he was off flying only temporarily and recovering
from being "badly shot up". Another officer remarked
that he looked fit enough and to this Prune replied "Ah
yes, old horseman, but you see I'm actually so full of
enemy metal that until the docs remove some of it I
cannot fly because it actually puts my compass out".

AIRBORNE AGAIN

His CO spent a long time wondering how the hell he
could get Prune posted and he went so far as to ply the
Station Intelligence Officer with brandies in an attempt to
have him accept Prune as "an acting Intelligence Officer"
but the wily I.O. was not that easily seduced and told the
Squadron Leader that Pilot Officer Prune couldn't even
act intelligently, let alone be an 'acting Intelligence
Officer'. Things happened fast in these days, however,
and by the time Prune reported for duty again his CO
had been shot down over France and taken prisoner.
Having had Percy for two months, he counted himself
fortunate, he "let well alone", and made absolutely no
attempt to escape.

Prune was never taken by the enemy though he came
close to it on one occasion. He'd been heard to boast in
the Mess that if ever he got caught by Jerry, the Luftwaffe
Intelligence blokes wouldn't get anything out of him. This
was safe to say — he didn't know anything. Back on
flying — acting as an inter-squadron messenger, he made
what was one of his rare good landings on what he
thought was Prangmere, after flying from Hornchurch —

where his aircraft had been repaired overnight after he had landed so badly on what he though was West Malling. There was a very heavy ground-mist over the field and this was just as well for, had be been able to see clearly, he may have ploughed in as usual. As it was, he had wasted an awful lot of time going round and round trying to find how to bring down the undercarriage of his Miles Magister, an aircraft which had a fixed undercarriage, the wheels being permanently down anyway.

The 'drome on which he landed was not Prangmere but Joinville, a French airfield then in enemy hands. A German 'erk', who must have been almost as dim as Prune, appeared out of the mist at Prune's elbow and Percy, a stickler for good appearances — as long as they weren't his own, noted that the mechanic's tunic was unbuttoned and he ticked him off for being slovenly. Prune's tones, if not his words, brought this humble Hun up to attention and he promptly executed an artful move which must often have stopped German officers mid-sentence — he raised his arm and shouted "Heil Hitler". Prune then peered closer at the fellow and saw that what he'd taken to be an airman on "the Glasgow" squadron, "because", as he said later, "he talked so thickly", was in fact the Enemy! He gave his aircraft full boost and the tail unit caught the German and dragged him for a while over the airfield — unbuttoning the rest of his uniform, then Prune became airborne and later was seaborne on his aircraft which had run out of fuel. He was plucked from the plane just in time by a party of Rye fishermen and later (since they regaled him for hours in "The Ypres Tavern") he was returned to Prangmere.

After this he was posted to a bomber station in Scotland with indecent haste and not a few indecent words from his CO — to be as far away from the Battle of Britain as possible. Some say that the posting came direct from an office at Bentley Priory — from the Commander in Chief himself, who no doubt felt that while he and his pilots could take on and beat the Luftwaffe — Prune was an unneccessary additional risk.

After a brief interview with his Scottish Squadron-

Leader, it was decided that he could do with some extra navigation instructions (!) and a few days later he was sent on a navigational detail to the Midlands. On the way, he was ordered to return, but was told to "come back via Stratford to avoid deteriorating weather at Liverpool". He absorbed the first part of the message — about returning, but not the 'second part — about Stratford, until he was within ten minutes flying time from 'home' whereupon, his navigator recalling it, Prune determined not to drop any clangers on his new station, turned again and returned two hundred odd miles so that he could then, dutifully, fly back "via Stratford". As a result he ran out of fuel and force-landed his bomber in a potato field.

Shortly after this he was issued a pair of very dark tinted goggles with instructions to wear them so that his eyes would become accustomed to darkness as he was due to take part in a series of night-flying training flights. On the first of these exercises he made ten fruitless efforts to land the aircraft then his instructor, in despair, took over and put the aircraft down. On landing, the instructor ordered Percy to seek out the Medical Officer as soon as possible to have a night vision test and he left his pupil to veer off into the gloom toward the flight hut like a blind man. After Percy had felt his way to the hut — and around it several times before finding the door, he was seen by another pilot to be still wearing the dark-tinted goggles which, while they enabled one to see one's way around in daylight, rendered one utterly blind at night.

On his second night flight he narrowly missed taking his aircraft and himself right into a loch when, losing his way entirely, he cast about for some sort of guiding light and perceived a red one on his left and this he made for, turning in tight circles and keeping his eye on the little red light all the time. He had actually lost 2,000 feet and was on the point of taking his craft right into the chill black waters of a huge loch when he realised that what he'd been making for was in fact the red, port navigation light on his own wing tip.

His Scottish 'Father' decided to allow Percy to fly only as a passenger after this and until he, the CO, could think up something. Percy was taken up by another pilot and instructor and told to sit in the rear of an Oxford which was up on a daylight exercise over the Scottish moors. On completion of a period of instrument flying, at around 3,000 feet, the instructor glanced round to find that Prune had vanished — the aircraft was empty. Four days later Prune got off a bus outside the main gate of his station, his parachute container and harness tucked under his arm, and the canopy trailing behind him. To his CO, who had been conducting a search for him but had finally (and gleefully) given him up for lost, Prune explained that, "feeling like a leak", he'd opened the door of the aircraft to relieve himself and had fallen out.

It was on this occasion that a Commanding Officer risked being cashiered by forging the signature of an Air Vice Marshal — to get Percy posted. Other means were tried from time to time so that he was posted and passed, like a Whitehall buck, not only from station to station, but from Command to Command and this time he fetched up at the School of Air Support. From here he was sent by a sanguine Squadron Leader to carry out a low-level strafing exercise on a West Country site and for this he was 'bombed up' with dummy bombs. His navigation was as shaky as ever (he said afterwards that his "compass was out!") and he was once again reported to be flying over Occupied France — over a dummy airfield laid out by the fiendishly clever Hun near the village of St Praline de Prangue. Prune didn't hesitate here. He made a commendable job of strafing the field to destroy several ply-wood and canvas Messerschmidts but unfortunately he ran out of fuel on his return to base and came down in the Channel — which rather surprised him because he thought he'd been over the River Severn. He was returned to his station by courtesy of the Air Sea Rescue Service and, facing his CO, he confidently expected to be highly commended for displaying initiative and individual enterprise — perhaps to be recommended for the DFC, for strafing this enemy installation, even though he'd got there by mistake. He was informed that St Praline's was a dummy 'drome, designed expressly to receive as many real British bombs as possible —

designed expressly for clots like him who risked their aircraft — not to mention their lives, to go into 'action' against a set of theatrical props. When Prune had thought this over he brightened and said "Oh well, Sir, not to worry eh! They were, after all, only *dummy* bombs". This kind of abortive action, misapplied endeavour, which could include the dropping of all your real bombs in the right place but losing your aircraft through some stupid oversight on the way back — or achieving the destruction of an enemy plane at the cost of your own, came in time to be referred to as a 'Prunic Victory'.

Typical examples of these abortive war-efforts of his were seen later in the war. Percy was sent off on a Channel patrol with orders to drop depth charges on or near enemy submarines. Needless to say he never saw a U-boat but, bearing in mind that such explosives as those he carried were very expensive, he decided to jettison them before he returned to base in such a way as not to cost the British Government too much — he dropped them with dramatic effect in a field behind a railway station on a branch line in Dorset. Asked to account for this extraordinary action, Percy unblushingly explained that he'd felt that they'd be easier to recover if he dropped them on the land, whereas they'd have "sunk without trace at sea" and "could never have been used again". Flying with a Mosquito squadron for a brief, very brief, spell, he pressed home his attacks on Nazi objectives with the best of them but while the other pilots straddled their targets with bombs, Prune surprised the enemy by dropping his reserve fuel wing-tanks in a low level attack and then returned home with his bomb load intact.

"Willing but wet, dutiful but dumb".

Back at Prangmere, his old squadron Intelligence Officer got wind of the fact that Prune was about to be returned. The CO started to pull strings like a puppeteer working overtime and got the whole shoot, the Squadron, posted to the Far East.

It was another Squadron-Leader at Prangmere who found out about Percy the hard way and, in despair, he relegated him to the job of Duty Pilot but took the precaution of putting two astute aircraftsmen at his "command", ostensibly, that is, but in fact, since they knew the job backwards, the CO felt that they'd save Prune from his greater idiocies. The job of Duty Pilot involved watching aircraft landing and taking off, reporting arrivals and departures, from a hut in front of the hangars on the edge of the flying-field and reporting everything to the Operations Room. One aspect of this job appealed to Percy no end — it was the firing off of green or red Verey cartridges from a pistol and the two aircraftsmen allowed him to do this while they concerned themselves with the more technical side of the job but one morning, when one airman had got a special forty-eight hour pass "to attend a family funeral", but was in fact on his way to the classic boose-up of a family wedding, and the other 'erk' had 'gone sick' with what he called 'the squitters', due no doubt to his having worked with Percy for a fortnight, Prune was left on his own until replacements could be sent over from HQ.

The Battle of Britain had been fought and won but soon the aerodrome — the field of Prangmere, took on much the same aspect as it had had during those violent days. A little Miles Magister, which had been taxying sedately across the field, was being importuned in the most embarrassing fashion by a Hurricane which, signalled in by Prune, had dropped out of the sky like some randy old cock-bird and almost mounted 'Maggie'. A Blenheim, at 700 feet, was doing something that Blenheims — twin-engined bombers, were never designed to do — a 'Victory Roll' — to avoid a Spitfire which had taken off, hell for leather, (after Percy's OK,) just beneath it. Just to add the right authentic touch, 'A' Flight hut was being evacuated with considerable urgency by a dozen aircraftsmen and pilots who'd formed a gambling school there, because it was well alight from a 'safe Green' which Percy, emulating Wyatt Earp had fired from the hip, and sent horizontally through one of the windows.

For a Duty Pilot his powers of observation were lamentably poor. One day he did manage to notice three aircraft standing outside the hangars and later saw that one was taxied out and then took off — this being a serviceable plane which had just been taken out of the hangar after an overhaul. Tongue protruding, Percy duly logged the take-off of this aircraft and while he was thus engaged the other two aircraft were trundled into the hangar by the mechanics for *their* repair and inspection so that when Percy came out of his hut again they had disappeared. Without enquiring further he re-entered his hut and not only logged them as airborne but he also 'cooked' their take-off times and call-signs so that, late that night, Command was frantically trying to trace two missing aircraft — pilot's names unknown, aircraft which were in fact at that time cosily stabled in the darkened hangars resting their weary props and flaps during a thirty-hour inspection.

That Service phrase 'thirty-hour inspection' once tripped Prune but then so did many an RAF term which was not purely social or smutty. The phrase indicated an inspection which was carried out on all aircraft every thirty hours of their flying. Percy asked the officer, whom he always referred to as 'The Plumber', who should have been addressed as the Engineer Officer, when *his* aircraft would be ready and that officer told him that it was in for a "thirty-hour". Percy said tersely that 'The Plumber' had better "put more bods to work on it" *because* he wanted it in a shorter time than *that*. Prune was an amiable character but could be terse with any who did not respect his commission, although he was downright casual toward officers of a higher rank than his own — especially if they didn't sport the wings of aircrew, and when he asked a mechanic at a bench in the hangar what job he was doing and the 'erk' replied "I'm repairing a prop-boss", Percy said icily "Please address me as sir, airman, not 'boss' ".

Prune not only failed constantly to do the right thing, he rarely said the right thing — invariably saying the wrong one. He was sent to Headquarters Fighter Command to be the recipient of a 'rocket' from a Very Superior Officer and, rounding a Nissen hut at Bentley Priory, he fetched up with a large Waaf sergeant. The blouse and slacks of battle-dress had only just been issued

Waaf personnel — hitherto it had been issued only to the RAF and, coming up with this beefy person Prune prodded and remarked, "Funny place to wear your Mae West, Sergeant, *under* your blouse!" The Waaf, a Physical Training Instructress, drew off and fetched Prune a clout which almost put him out.

Among many tactless remarks which Percy made from time to time perhaps the oddest was that which he addressed to a high ranking Service padre in a bar at the Dorchester. The padre held no less a rank than that of Air Commodore and, turning chattily to this lofty man of God, Percy enquired in matey fashion what the gentleman had done "in Civvy Street".

Percy's talent for shooting a line was only surpassed by his ability to justify his most outrageous errors.

"INTO THE WIDE BLUE YONDER"

It isn't easy to select a "typical prunery" from the pile of reports of Boards of Enquiry and Courts Martial which Prune attended as the central figure over the war years but perhaps his brush with Mussolini's anti-aircraft defences, when he was flying out of Malta as the pilot of a Blenheim, may be taken as a run of the mill sort of day for Prune on Ops. It was as well that he was, on this occasion, what was known, in the elegant parlance of RAF flight huts, as "Arse-End Charlie", when the squadron was ordered off on a raid on Sicily — that there was no one taking off behind him. It always unnerved pilots to be behind Prune's aircraft and the order of their going was no accident — it was found by the Squadron Leader that, because of an odd tendency for Prune to fire off his guns at that moment when he should have been selecting 'wheels up', pilots were also nervous of flying in front of him, and so a very rapid take-off of the whole flight was thus effected. Many a pilot flying in Prune's vicinity frequently wished that there was much more sky.

'C for Clot', Prune's aircraft, sped across the field (he should of course have been on the runway), with his crew expecting to be airborne at any moment — when the engines lost power and he taxied on at speed and into some long grass at the edge of the field. Here he ran over three ankles — both those of a Sub-Lieutenant in the Fleet Air Arm and one of those of a blonde Wren, who was known in RN ward-rooms as "Scarper Flo' ". From his sick-bay bed later, the Sub-Lieutenant, Swingit by name, said that he and Flo' had been lying there in the grass discussing the history of the Royal Navy and he had just got to explaining the meaning of the phrase, "The Nelson Touch", when the port wheel of the Blenheim ran over their ankles.

Prune hauled in 'C for Clot', with a shriek of brakes, within eighteen inches of a thick hedge and an ominous silence settled over the aircraft. This was broken by Sergeant Winde who politely asked his captain — "What bollixed that up?"

Winde had been sitting in his turret, tensed up, with his eyes shut and fingers crossed. "All under control, old horseman!" said Prune. "Simply forgot to close our gills and put down flaps".

The sergeant uncrossed his fingers and opened his eyes, or it might have been the other way round, while Flying Officer Fixe, an RC, simply crossed and re-crossed himself — for the twentieth time. Prune's air-gunner had only one thing for which he could thank Prune — just before he was appointed gunner in 'C for Clot' he had been suffering from an obstinate concretion which brought him within an ace of being remustered into a ground job. Within twenty-four hours of flying with Prune, however, his chronic constipation was relieved and he was fast developing the most sensitive 'twitch' in Bomber Command, or, for that matter, the whole 'Air Works'.

'C for Clot' was hauled off the hedge by Works Flight and Prune then received belated orders cancelling his joining the original flight and telling him to simply take off (actually the Controller did not say "take" off) — on "a reconnaisance flight". This time, after a thorough cock-pit check, Prune achieved a take-off which actually took 'C for Clot' right off — behaving only a little like an elderly eider duck with a strangulated hernia, although this success was marred by Prune failing to take up his undercarriage until well out of sight of Malta. He recced for a while and at one point he indicated "Bandits at three o'clock" and yelled at Sergeant Winde to fire on them. The gunner desisted because before Prune had seen them, Winde had recognised these "Messerschmidt Jaguars" as the returning Blenheims of that flight with which they should now have been flying.

Getting bored with stooging, Prune decided that they should return to base and this gave his crew another hazard on which to ponder. If there was anything more terrifying than taking off with Prune at the controls — it was landing with him, so that simply being shot at by the enemy in between came as something of a welcome interlude.

Flying Officer Fixe gave him a course which he ignored because, he said, he could make it back to base with his eyes shut and that is why he fetched up over the toe of Italy after being almost forcibly restrained from landing on an airstrip in enemy-occupied Sicily. The Italians' great guns were going that way and making the sky around 'C for Clot' resemble nothing so much as Edwardian sea-side boarding-house wall-paper — with great bursts of crimson and orange set in puffs of dirty brown 'foliage'. Making a wide turn through this and by now accepting his navigator's advice, Prune was able to get back to Malta with his fuel gauge registering *pints*. He wisely decided to jettison his bombs before attempting a landing. This he did with remarkable effect, between two anchored British cruisers!

The flare path was laid out by this time and Percy, ignoring the neccessity of getting a 'green' signal, or even selecting a run-way to land on, came in, downwind, and across the path of three night-fighters which were taking off. These 'cat's-eyes' were forced to describe a perfect 'Prince of Wales' Feathers' high above the 'drome, as Prune touched down on a rock-pile, while the aerodrome, with red cartridges bursting all over the area and Aldis lamps frantically flashing red, looked like the celebration of Joe Stalin's birthday in Moscow.

Miraculously surviving the roughage of the rock-pile, Prune slewed 'C for Clot' in a tight turn and went on over

the bumpy ground until Sergeant Winde yelled out a
warning. They were making at a fair clip toward a fully
bombed-up Wellington. As this huge, four-engined job
loomed up in front of Percy's plane, ground staff and
aircrew could be seen running away from it in terror.
Percy saw it just in time to apply standard brake and
then he opened up his starboard engine with a roar, his
wing just slicing off one of the 'Wimpy's' port-outer
propeller blades. 'C for Clot' then turned and headed for
the open field again.

As he throttled back his starboard motor, which was
still roaring, there was a fiery belching-out of flame from
the exhaust which, under the circumstances, was a
normal occurrence, but Percy thought that 'C for Clot'
was about to burst into flames. He didn't lose his head,
however, he was aware of the traditional role of a captain
in a doomed ship — when the safety of his crew should
be his first consideration, and he bravely screamed
"Everybody out!" and, scrambling out of the cock-pit, he
shuffled on his backside down the mainplane to fall
untidily, but safely, on the ground before his crew could
even extricate themselves from their seat harness. 'C for
Clot' went on pilotless, crazily turning round and round
in a giddy fashion, until it fetched up with its starboard
engine right over a blazing oil drum which had been set
out as part of the flare-path. Prune's crew were seen to
pop out of the aircraft in different directions as the
Blenheim appeared to erupt and by the brilliant light of
its burning, Fixe and Winde were picked up and carried
to hospital and Pilot Officer Prune was picked up and led
away under close arrest.

CHAIR-BORNE

One form of punishment meted out to erring bird-men
was that of making them chair-borne and posting them
for a term to Air Ministry. Prune was eventually sent to
Kingsway to allow the British aircraft factories to step up
production and replace those aircraft he had rendered
'unserviceable'. In short order he found himself in a tiny
office where, it was thought, he could do no harm, but he

did. He managed to smash two model aircraft which
another 'caged bird' had passed his time making in the same office.

During the first two days other caged-birds would put their heads around the door and say something like "Well, blow me down, our Percy of all people!" and go away laughing but on the third day a 'wingless wonder', with three rings up, looked in and, seeing Percy quite unoccupied, he said "Ah, want some work old man?" and retreated before Percy could correçt that unfortunate impression. Within two days Percy's horizon, as far as he could see, was entirely bounded by files, which a Mr Perusalle, a Higher Clerical Officer of the Branch, had unloaded on him. In vain Prune tried to get rid of them but they were invariably brought back because he'd written the wrong things on them. Mr Perusalle would explain gently that Prune had signed his name in red ink, which was strictly reserved for Members of the Air Council when "Viewing with Displeasure" — or something, and Mr P would mention tactfully that the calm and dignified flow of a minute required phrasing such as "As a result of which error of judgement on the part of the pilot the aircraft must now be considered a total wreck" and not "The pilot dropped a clanger and the kite went for a shit".

PO Prune tried to organise his little office — in his 'IN' tray there were files which he labelled "Too secret for words" and "Not to be opened by anybody at all"; in his 'OUT' tray there was an empty gin bottle set tidily on top of a photograph of Rita Hayworth with the caption "Whacko Perc' — get in there, it's your solo" — in his handwriting. Still the files kept coming in but most of them were Greek to the simple Percy. Not that he could always be blamed for not catching on because, as the Allied Forces were driving hard across Western Europe in an effort to reach the Third Reich and force the Enemy to play his final fixture 'at home', the Civil Service was in no particular hurry. Prune would receive such memoes as

Consideration has been given to the method of naming variants of the basic types of aircraft, in order to simplify the allocation of designations and reduce the number of marks the significance of which has to be memorised. In future, variants developed from a basic type for a different operational purpose will be distinguished, as a normal rule, by a combination of basic name and a letter or letters appropriate to the operational role. To avoid the possibility of confusion (!) the original type from which the variant is derived will similarly be differentiated. Each variant type will have its letter(s) appropriate to its operational role, to distinguish significant changes in performance or interchangeability, as hitherto. It is not practical to keep lateral correspondence between mark number and leading features of variant and original types, and such correspondence is not to be presumed.

From this kind of gobbledegook a sharper mind may have eventually perceived that this meant, in effect, "Aircraft will be given a name for each basic type with a letter or letters added for each variant", and would certainly have been easily taken in the slow stride of a "genned-up type" — but for Percy who, in a mixed Officers' Mess, often went through the door marked "WAAF Personnel" instead of the 'Gents' (marked "RAF Personnel",) it was Double Dutch and so he decided to chuck the whole thing up and go on leave for a spell. Here he made a serious tactical error. Hoping that if his office were unoccupied people wouldn't bring 'things' to it, he put in for his leave and tooled off to Prune Parva for seven days.

What Percy didn't know was that a temporarily unoccupied office in a Ministry attracts files like bees to honey. Word of an unguarded dumping ground went the rounds of the corridors and along the stained bars of foetid little drinking clubs around the Covent Garden area and up the marble bars of the old Holborn Hotel and the Waldorf like wild fire and every file that no other caged bird wanted, files which nobody could put away — because they required "A Decision in Writing", came flocking in to Prune's office like homing pigeons so that when he got back from his leave, with a chronic hangover, he couldn't get into his office until he'd managed to execute a half flick roll through the half-opened door to make a typically untidy landing against the legs of his chair. He began to look over that huge pile of files. After a day or two he had one of those rare flashes of animal cunning, the kind of brief spark of inspiration noted as a spasmodic characteristic in the long line of Prunes — probably the only characteristic which

has enabled them to *be* a long line, and certainly the only one which had brought Prune through the war so far.

For the first time in his service at Air Ministry he got in early for three mornings running. He ineptly lettered a notice OUT OF ODOUR (last word intended as ORDER) and this he hung on one of the cubicle doors in the Ministry 'Gents' and then spent from half past eight until opening time tearing up the contents of dozens of files and pulling the chain on them.

He then obtained a list of Polish and Czechoslovakian officers who were on Air Ministry or Command duty and, working steadily through the list from A to Z (and there were a surprising number of the latter), he sent one of his files to each of them so that within a week he'd got rid of the lot — all, that is, except one. Because of its incredible girth, this great file had come to be known in the corridors of Adastral House and Princes House as "Jumbo" and Prune had it despatched to a Polish officer who was the last on his list and then he put on his cap with the air of one who has successfully completed a very difficult job and went off to The Waldorf for "a lunch hour thrash". As he stood drinking, boasting and boring other caged birds at the bar, he was secretly smiling at the probable reactions of that Flight-Lieutenant Tomas Zvuvevski on getting the last file which, as if it did not already look as though it was horribly constipated, was chock full of bumph, memoes, minutes and plans giving stercoraceous details of what to do with human waste on temporary airfields by the construction of field lavatories and the digging and screening of such temporary 'lavs' as that one which was dubbed, lyrically, "The Icelandic Lily — Mark 4".

Having "got the taste" in the bar of the Waldorf, Percy went back after his liquid lunch to put in for what he described as a "semi-official" leave, at the same time backing up his case with the quite truthful assertion that there was, at that moment, no work on his desk. He intended to "dot down" to Biggin Hill to visit a pal serving on a squadron there.

Prune's friend was 'not at home' — in fact, at the moment when Prune drove through the Main Gate, his friend was dicing about over the Channel with what *must* have been the very last Messerschmidt of Goering's Western Command. To get what he called, "a nostalgic whiff of the old high octane", Prune prevailed on a gullible officer in charge of the 'Works Flight' to let him take up a trainer plane — "for a spot of circuits and bumps". He flew around Biggin Hill for a while and at one point almost collided with his friend who was then returning to base, very frightened but triumphant, and with his aircraft shot full of holes. After nearly killing this pal of his, Prune flew off toward the coast, and coming out of low cloud, he caught sight of an aircraft flying toward him. He peeled off to avoid a head-on collision. As he went down he saw that the aircraft bore the ominous Swastika and Cross — but the pilot hadn't fired on him! Prune's aircraft was, of course, unarmed, and he thought that either the enemy had gallantly desisted or had himself run out of ammunition. This inspired Prune to emulate the chivalrous flyers of the Royal Flying Corps in the First World War and he turned to fly alongside the enemy craft and was peering at it to locate the pilot, so that he could gallantly salute him, when 'The Hun' went into cloud — Prune followed.

When Percy emerged from the cloud he saw the German craft below — it was now diving and Prune thought "Ah, poor fellow, he's in trouble". He then thought that it would be no end of a feather in his cap if he went down and landed alongside and took the enemy pilot prisoner. He pushed his 'stick' forward and chased down after the 'bandit' which seemed about to touch down in a potato field — which it did, and then promptly blew up with an immense explosion which took off Percy's starboard mainplane and twisted his tattered aircraft upside down so that he crashed, in his turn — into the centre of a large clump of blackthorn.

When Prune got out of the aircraft and the bushes — looking like the sole survivor of a bayonet charge, he peered around for the enemy plane but it had quite disappeared and all he saw was a large crater where it had landed. This was to be expected for he'd escorted, and then closed in to try landing alongside, a V1 Flying Bomb.

Rather than face the Biggin Hill Works Flight Officer, he sloped off across the field and caught a bus which got him over the border into Sussex.

Percy had driven to Biggin in his Lagonda which he'd bought while up at Cambridge before the war, and had used it throughout the war sometimes carrying ten or twelve bods at a time, and running it on high octane aircraft fuel, which he'd risked a Court Martial to obtain, had impaired its performance and although he had a certain amount of sentimental regard for the old bus, — Percy never did go back for it and, for all we know, it may be ranged up opposite that famous Spitfire at the Main gate of Biggin Hill to this day.

DEMOB'

The day at last came for Prune's release from the Royal Air Force and the fact that he was demobbed in good order and not slung out on his neck, is an example of the colossal luck of the Prunes. He even mucked this up, however, and spent ages sitting at a desk opposite a Sergeant under whose patient directions he was filling in the innumerable forms required. The Sergeant, though a patient fellow, was simply hanging on for the moment when Prune ceased to be an officer so that he could stop calling him "Sir" and call him at least one of those things which kept occuring to him. Prune trailed from room to room and from floor to floor with his forms, getting his medical examination here and travelling allowance home there, until he was giddy. He became so confused that at one point he was actually out of the Air Force and could have gone home but he went out of a ground floor door into a yard for a smoke and a pause in the confusing business then throwing away the fag-end, he re-entered and, by some extraordinary fluke, signed up for another ten years service!

Fortunately for the peace-time RAF, this mistake was soon discovered and Prune emerged to commence his blind stroll down Civvy Street.

He tried a variety of jobs but few details are available
except in the case of that contretemps which came about
from his being given the job of car salesman in a swank
West-End showrooms. He lost this situation as the result
of an offer he made to take the prospective buyer of a
Jaguar for a trial run around Mayfair. He seated his
prospect comfortably, made a thorough 'cock-pit' check,
started up, restrained himself from doing his normal
excessive revving up of the engine, then drove the new car
straight through the plate-glass windows of the
showrooms, across Piccadilly and fetched up with a
squealing of the brakes — *and* a squealing of the
prospective customer, under the portico of the Ritz Hotel.
He backed out of this, into the path of a double-decker
bus, and then drove down St James' against the flow of
one-way traffic, to screech to a halt within eighteen inches
of the highly polished toe-caps of the boots of a
Grenadier Guardsman on duty outside St James' Palace.
His passenger afterwards told me that the guardsman, no
doubt as imperturbable as any of his fellows in the
Brigade, went as white as death and that the fur on his
bearskin cap actually stood on end.

When I was told this story I decided to seek out Prune
to see how well he was coping with the complexities of
civilian life. I had also heard that he'd had a stroke of
luck.

An obscure great-uncle, who emigrated to the States in
1885, had become known in the Old West as Panhandle
Prune — not, of course, because he came from the Texas
Panhandle but because he was for years a pan-handler,
actually living on his wits which, for a Prune, is a very
precarious existence. Panhandle purchased some
apparently worthless land on which he tried to raise
apples but although his trees grew to a prodigious size,
they never bore any fruit and then, in 1950, when he was
far too old, at eighty-nine, to enjoy his good fortune, oil
was discovered on his property. It was ironical that on the
day he received his first payment for the oil yield all his
trees burst into heavy blossom. This resulted in a bumper
crop from those apple trees which still remained,
scattered around the oil rigs.

Panhandle was too mean to employ help, despite his wealth, and he took to going out and picking up the fallen fruit and selling it from a stall on the state highway. Unfortunately while he was engaged in picking up his windfalls one day a wind rose and a tree fell — across his neck. After a long search for an heir, Percy got *his* windfall and a local newspaper reports him as making a profound remark about it — "Squire Prune said 'Well, it's an ill wind that has no turning".

Percy knows little or nothing about oil — in fact, while waiting for his car to be filled up with petrol at a garage, he once expressed to me his admiration for "garage people who always know where to put those things (the petrol pumps) over the place where the stuff will be". He was, however, planning to go and see the property that Panhandle had left him when, with a sound like bath water going down the plug-hole, the wells stopped slurping and dried up completely. Still Percy had received enough money under old Panhandle's will to enable him to drop out of the rat race and, as the hereditary Squire of Prune Parva, to retire there and live the life of a country gentleman and indulge in some harmless and utterly unprofitable farming. I decided to go and see him.

Prune Parva

SUSSEX

When I first wrote to ask Prune whether I could come and visit his ancestral home I had already decided that it would be appropriate to go by air. This was just as well because the village is practically inaccessible any other way. Prune wrote back and said that this was a "Wizard idea" and that there was an excellent "runway actually in the village".

Flying west along the South Coast until we were over the Witterings, we turned inland and following the course, the wayward course, of the River Drivel and discovered the village in a gentle fold of the Downs.

Prune Parva, I found, forms a distinct 'plus' sign with the three principle buildings — Ineyne Manor, at the northern tip of the sign, St Dementia's Church in the bottom left-hand angle of it, and the Mug and Finger Inn in the bottom right hand angle. For the rest, the village is simply a scattering of cottages and shops.

From the air it is still possible to see the scars of war on the Downs, made as far back as 1940, and, with some sharp memories of that time, my pilot flew the little trainer high over turf which still bears signs of old bomb craters where, by accident or design, or in an effort to lighten his load and flee, some enemy pilot had dropped his bombs. Over Prune Parva we saw more signs of the destruction of yesteryear. There are the ruins of three cottages, the rubble of a 'fainting house' at the rear of the church, the remains of a gazebo on the south wall of the Manor's home-park and a couple of crater scars on the west side of the home-farm. Back in 1943 the peace of a summer Sunday afternoon was shattered when an aircraft, coming from the coast, flew low over the old village and dropped its bomb load right across it.

Despite repeated warnings and threats from his CO, Percy Prune had *again* come over to "give the old place a beat-up" but, while attempting to show off to his family and the villagers, he had, inevitably, pressed the wrong tit and almost wiped out his family seat.

History, which is mainly concerned with bloody events, has consigned Prune Parva to centuries of happy obscurity and, except when Percy is around, a peace unbroken. According to one monkish chronicle, the Parva has existed since the year 716 when Ethel the Bald granted the Manor to Abbot Erewigge but it passed into the possession of the Prunes, along with its warrens, fishponds, mill, hides, hundreds, berewicks and wapen-takes, before the Conquest. Even the branch-line railways which once ran some miles to the north and south of the village were axed by the Chairman of the Board of British Railways and, other than ancient salt-ways and packhorse paths, no road of any importance has ever run through. The main thoroughfare, the upright of our 'plus' sign, is really the termination of a secondary road which once connected with a main road to the coast. The village is therefore practically inaccessible by road but should some wayward traveller manage to get down the various cart tracks and holloways to the Parva, he would enter the village over a narrow bridge, spanning a near-stagnant brook, marked with a fading notice UNSAFE FOR ANY VEHICLES, and would then continue up the High Street to come to the cross-roads, with the church on his left and the inn on his right. Skirting a huge oak set on a green in the centre of the road, he would then proceed up until he came to the gates of Ineyne Manor.

The road which crosses this main road to form our 'plus' sign was laid down in 1901 by Prune's grandfather, Phillip. It starts in a thick copse called Peeper's Wood and goes over the main road to finish at the brink of a water-filled chasm euphemistically referred to locally as the "Water Splash". Grandfather Phillip had temporarily switched his interest from cars to steam-rollers and after purchasing one of these monsters, he had this useless road made up to go out of the wood and cross the main road to finish at the 'splash' — he almost finished himself in the 'splash'. He spent several weeks tarring and happily rolling the road, intending to use it later as a car-racing track, but he was discouraged from this rolling up and down by the village blacksmith whose dog and left foot he had squashed and, in an effort to dodge the heavy tongs and hammers thrown at him by the smithy's huge son, who was acting in a rather hysterical manner, Phillip drove his steam roller at speed up his road and right over the brink of the "Water Splash". He escaped drowning by climbing from the submerged cabin and up the chimney stack. In certain lights, between the clumps of water-cress, it is still possible to glimpse this great vehicle rusting away at the bottom.

We circled the village looking for that "runway" which Percy had written about and finally came to the conclusion that what he had meant was this odd stretch of road of Phillip's which, for some obscure reason, has come to be known as Shagger's Chase. It took some careful flying to put our trainer down just beyond Peepers Wood and still not fetch up with the aircraft's prop boss boring through the trunk of the huge oak at the cross-roads.

The isolation of Prune Parva on what is, in effect, a peninsula, girdled by slow-flowing or downright stagnant waters, has limited the growth and development of Prune Parva, while the very nature of those foetid pools and sluggish rivulets and their seeping into the wells of the village water supply, has seriously affected the growth and the development of the villagers themselves. The population has rarely exceeded 150 souls and this figure has only been maintained by the insatiable lust of the men of the village and the wanton nature of Parva women and girls because while visitations of the Black Death and Bubonic have sent only eight locals to the churchyard over the centuries, typhoid has accounted for hundreds.

When we had landed and looked around we agreed that Prune Parva was a veritable film-set village. The setting for some pretty, romantic film of country life made back in the late 1920s and, since then, left to decay on the film-lot. This obvious neglect, and the fact that it is all but inaccessible by any vehicle less than a tank, has produced in the place a self-sufficient, self-supporting, self-centred, suspicious and downright unfriendly community which has inter-married to a point of incest.

The cracked bell of St Dementia's clock struck "opening time". Ten minutes later the discordant clang of the clock over the stables up at Ineyne Manor indicated the same. Almost immediately a roar was heard from that direction and a vintage Lagonda came lurching wildly out of the gates and down the road at a furious rate to pull up in a cloud of dust within eighteen inches of the oak tree's trunk. Percy stepped out and greeted us effusively and immediately steered us toward the open door of the Mug and Finger Inn.

Percy certainly looked the part of a country gentleman. He had on a deerstalker hat of blinding check, a heavy tweed shirt and his old St Finga's tie, which of course he is entitled to wear, an Old Burks Hunt waistcoat with brass buttons — to which he is not entitled, cord breeches and Newmarket boots. His most outstanding garment, however, was a Norfolk jacket of such startling a pattern that it might have been cut from a horse blanket. It was fitted with heavy leather gun-butt patches — not only on the right shoulder but on the left as well, and leather bar-leaning patches running up from the cuffs to well beyond the elbows. This impressive garment was fitted with leather buttons the size of walnuts.

From behind the bar of the Mug and Finger we were greeted by the Parva's "John Barleycorn" — the village "Boniface", Mr Bert Ullidge, with a glare of intense hatred and suspicion. He served up three pints of cloudy, ill-kept beer in stony silence and we settled down to look around the famous hostelry which is hardly changed from the days when Prune's ancestress, Joan Gotobed, served there in medieval times. It is a 'free house' in more ways than one since it practically never closes and whereas in other taverns one may hear the plea "Is there time for one before you close?", at 'the Mug' you will often hear "Is there time for another before you open?" It wasn't very full when we entered — just two villagers, one collapsed under a bench to our left and another asleep in the fireplace with his head up the chimney. Ullidge is, however, able to restrain the villagers from their greater excesses by the dreadful threat of "barrin" — for to be barred from here would mean virtual banishment from the village since there is not another pub' for some fifteen miles around.

The Mug and Finger is an old, erratic, low-ceiling tavern which is entirely appropriate to its old, erratic, low-browed keeper. The floor of the bar is stone-flagged and footworn while the woodwork is riddled with worm and the parlour at the back has such variations of floor level as will trip the unwary visitor or even, since the boards are rotten, actually collapse under him and trap or break his legs.

Bert Ullidge apparently encourages a cosy, close atmosphere a' nights because on the wall beside his bar is a densely fly-spotted notice which runs "Order your mug, light up your pipes — puff, and fug it!" In winter, what with the rancid shag of the locals and the smoke from a fire, the chimney of which hasn't been swept since the Restoration, it is quite impossible to see your mug before your face. When Glad', Ullidge's consort, decides to have a matey drink with the customers *"that* side of the bar", it isn't possible to move, even if you can see, because Glad' is not merely the "comfortable body" which Prune described her, she can't be called fat — she is obese to a point of absurdity. Glad' and Bert, Prune told us, met in a most romantic manner during the First World War. Bert was serving in a Labour Battalion into which he'd been recruited after a chase by the Military Police over Groper's Green at the back of what was then his father's pub'. He later became a patient in a military hospital, a V.D. hospital, where Glad' was a nurse and her admiration for the young soldier soon ripened into love.

A large fading photograph of Ullidge, in uniform and handcuffed to a Military Policeman, hangs in a prominent place in the bar. We were quickly made aware of Mr Ullidge's pet hate. This is the vast old oak, which, in a guide book to the village, written by a curate of St Dementia's in 1913, is described as "shading the village inn" — in fact it menaces it. It seems all the time in imminent danger of falling on the 'Mug' and yet it obstinately burgeons every year, this, despite the quarts of acid and pounds of saltpetre, which, in the small hours, Ullidge pours into its bowels through a hole in the trunk to kill it.

The gnarled bark of the old tree's trunk is ravaged by time and deeply scored with obscene symbols and signs made by the village boys over the centuries. The bole is also viciously scarred where successive Prunes have gone past it, holus bolus, up to the Manor, either incapable of good driving or drunk — or both, hitting the tree with coach and carriage wheel hubs in early times and car wings and bumpers in later days. The tree has become an obsession with Ullidge. He is a patriotic man but modest about his war-time exploits, and he wants the tree removed and a war memorial "to the Parva's fallen" put up in its place.

Percy told us that both he, and his father before him, had been agreeable to supplying the actual memorial — a huge cylindrical column which has stood for the past one hundred and eighty odd years in a secluded part of his home park but the Rector of the Parva has always opposed this erection. We felt, when we saw it later, that this was not altogether surprising because the 'column', known as 'Paul's Pecker', was set up by Peter 'Beau' Prune to commemorate his short career as a monk at Medmenham Abbey. It was the work of a stone-mason who made it under the inspired direction of Sir Francis Dashwood of the 'Hell Fire Club' who had it erected at Wycombe as the dominating feature of his pornographic landscape garden.

Apart from 'Paul's Pecker' being a most inappropriate pillar for the memorial, any war memorial to the Parva's fallen would be rather bare of inscriptions because all but seven men of the village either evaded service or got excused on one pretext or another in both wars. Two of this seven were Percy and his father. They served, but didn't 'fall' — well, they fell out of the sky — frequently, but not fatally. The third was Bert Ullidge who spent practically all his 'service' in *that* hospital. The fourth enlisted as a cook but died of food poisoning in 1914. The fifth valorous Parvanian was trampled by a mule during embarkation for France in 1916 and the sixth was not a man but a mere boy. He was George Danglin who left the family business, which, a typical village work-shop, still bears the fading sign "Lowe & Danglin, Cobblers", to "go for a soldier in 1917". You will be told in the village, as we were, that "'E lied about 'is height and got into the Grenadier Guards", although by all accounts George was a near-midget. This lad served only a short time — twenty-eight days, for theft, in the 'Glasshouse' at Aldershot. After this he was killed by a train on the branch line as he walked along the track toward his home-village in an attempt to desert. The last of this "Magnificent Seven" died bravely in 1940 just before Dunkirk when gangrene set in from a self-inflicted wound.

Despite these obvious drawbacks, Ullidge persists in his efforts to have a war memorial in place of what he calls "That discrepit ole monster —that disgrace to the village" — the tree, but in this he is as obstinately opposed by someone whom he also calls "That discrepit ole monster — that disgrace to the village", the Reverend George Piseener, Rector of the Parva. Nobody knows how old the Rector is but it is known that his first job, as a curate at St Dementia's, was to christen the Prunes' ancient butler, Clotte.

Piseener's Path is a feature of the village which is always pointed out to visitors — otherwise they could trip and break an ankle in it. It is a deep rut which runs right across the road from the Rectory gate to the doorstep of the Mug and Finger. The Rector's gate bears a scrolled plate on which, by accident of the signwriter, his illiteracy, or design inspired by personal knowledge of the incumbent, are the words "The Rectumry". The padre of Prune Parva has only himself to blame if his reputation is tarnished because back before the last war he tried to form a choir but with such a small population he could only get three boys and, going about his parochial duties, Mr Piseener was frequently heard to mutter "I must have some boys" and the world and his wife — as far as the Parva was concerned, thought the worst of him.

George Piseener was innocent on this occasion but in 1945 when his Bishop paid an unexpected visit to St Dementia's, the Rector came very close to being unfrocked. His Grace found him at tea with an old friend of his Oxford days and both of them were wearing frocks!

We left the inn with most of our beer untouched, since it looked and tasted like flower vase water overdue for changing, when a breeze sprang up and wafted through the bar windows. Although it was a change from the odour of stale beer and coarse shag tobacco, it was not a welcome change since it brought with it the scent of the 400 year old 'Gents' immediately outside.

St. Dementia's

We walked warily alongside Piseener's Path, through the lychgate toward St Dementia's. The church is described in the guide book as an "architecturally remarkable building" — remarkable, we thought, for the fact that it had not fallen down long ago because it is bung full of worm and honeycombed by death-watch beetle where it is not affected by dry rot — even the masonry Prune told us, is "full of stone-chats". Stepping around the large bits of masonry and pinnacles, which have broken off and fallen through the roof on to the stone flags of the aisle, Percy Prune led us toward the South Chapel which contains his family's tombs.

On the way Percy pointed out the 'Squire's Box Pew'. This, a relic of the old times, is a high, four-sided pew in which the Lord of the Manor of bygone times could attend public worship and yet not be stared at by the rude peasantry. Students of church architecture may be interested to know that the Prune box-pew is not merely a four-sided box. It is some seven feet high, and fitted with a heavy oak lid, within easy reach of the officiating clergyman. The Prunes have always been notorious for the discordancy of their singing voices and when the horrible noise from the Squire's pew became too unbearable, the parson could lean over, shut the lid and drown it.

In the South Chapel we saw the Prunes' Crusader tomb. In a niche, bearing the inscription "Drunk is he who prostate lies — without the power to drink or rise", is an urn which contains the ashes of that Prune of the Napoleonic campaigns, Major Pritchard Prune. The urn is made in the shape of a large bottle of Napoleon Brandy and bears the pithy inscription "85% PROOF".

There are several interesting brasses here including that of Sir Percivalle Prune (1315-1370) and the memorial of an old brass of the middle 15th century — Lady Portia Prunne. Percy told us that St Dementia's has now only two bells, a tenor and a treble, both cracked, but there used to be more. There was, for instance, a sanctus bell but it fell down during bell-ringing practise back in 1843.

One night the ringers were practising their Plains, Treble
Bobs, Grandsire Triples and Surprises but the greatest surprise of all was that of a certain choir boy, Bertie Byeblowe, who was standing immediately beneath the belfry when the sanctus bell dropped away from its worm-eaten hanging and fell down to cap him as neatly as a pea under a walnut shell. The sanctus bell had no tongue — it had been a dumb-bell for decades, and so Bertie was not seriously injured although the accident rendered him permanently round shouldered and bow-legged.

The organ is now quite unserviceable — it has been since 1930 when, after a silence of some years during which time nobody could be found to play it, a guest up at the Manor who confessed to what Percy called "orgiastic skill", answered the Rector's plea to come and play it for a wedding. To clear it, Prune's guest attempted a loud opening chord with all stops out and at the first great gusty gasp, the congregation was showered with hundreds of mice along with their litters and litter, which flew out of every aperture of the ancient instrument. Lady Priscilla Prune afterwards provided the church with a large radio-gram' (circa 1932) and also a selection of suitably pious records. Unfortunately some of Percy's records were accidentally included so that one Harvest Sunday the congregation were put about when the service was opened with the over-amplified voice of Sophie Tucker singing "My Yiddisher Momma". When the Verger hastily replaced it with another record they were treated to "Flat Foot Floosie with the Floy Floy".

Mention of the Verger, Mr Turnsodde, who divides his time, so Percy said, between being "Virgin, sextant and beetle", prompts us to say that no visitor should leave St Dementia's without seeing the church squint. It *belongs* to Mr Turnsodde. Combined with a tic, which makes his left eye give a most lascivious wink, the squint lends to his countenance a tricksy aspect quite out of keeping with his solemn tasks. Mr T's nickname in the village is 'Old Shagnasty'.

On leaving the church we were foolhardy enough to

accept Percy's offer of a lift in his Lagonda up to the great house — Ineyne Manor.

INEYNE MANOR

The treasure house of the Prunes dominates the Parva and is approached by a steep road up to the gates called Trollops Ride, though it is not certain whether this was named after the inventor of pillarboxes. As the gates are approached, the visitor gets something of a shock at the sight of a message in fading white-wash, on the red brick wall to his right. Prune explained that this was the work of Clotte, the butler, and it all started when his mother, Lady Priscilla, set out during the war to show our American allies some hospitality. She tried to emulate the Empress Eugenie by giving a series of *"Bals Americains"* and sent an invitation to the CO of an American airfield, some ten miles away, for he and his officers — along with their ladies, to come to a dinner-dance at Ineyne Manor.

Clotte was inevitably brought into this but he had a somewhat snobbish attitude to what he called "Colonials" and, on his night off, in the bar-parlour of the Mug and Finger, he was heard to express his disapproval of the bals Americaine — " 'Tisn't fittin' ", he opined, "for Lady Priscilla to go about 'olding American balls". When the Yanks, in convoy, pulled up at the manor gates, they got a shock. 'Old Glory' flew bravely alongside the Union Jack but in white letters, two feet tall, on the home-park wall, Clotte and the gardener had painted what they thought the lady of the house wanted there as a welcome and an indication that this was the right place — "BALLS AMERICANS!" The Yanks made a 'U' turn in Trollops Ride, went away and never came back — and Lady Priscilla never knew why.

Percy drove us up the drive which is flanked by ancient elms riddled with disease and falling down this way and that until we came to a huge one right across the road and were forced to leave the drive and proceed across the gardens which front the house. These gardens, Percy told us, were laid out by Brown — not, we hasten to add, the famous 'Capability' Brown but a certain Bert Brown who,

'ODD' MINIATURES AND INEYNE GHOSTS

COMTE DU PRALINE

SIR PRITCHARD PROON

'BEAU' PRUNE

CAPTAIN PERCY PRUNE

PELHAM PRUNE ESQ

SIR PLUMSTED PROON

MAJOR PRITCHARD PRUNE

as the village dipsomaniac, was known as 'Incapability' Brown. The crazy paving, crazy planting, lunatic landscaping and idiot bedding evidences this. 'Incapability' Brown fancied his chances as a topiarist, when in fact he was just a toper, so that whereas the trees of other great gardens are clipped into the shape of peacocks and things, those of the Prune gardens are in the shape of bottles of various well-known nineteenth century brands of whiskey, gin and brandy.

The gardens around the house are over that area once occupied by the moat. The moat is long gone. In the eighteenth century Pelham Prune was told that it would keep the Manor damp — in fact it was really the only means of keeping the foundations dry. Pelham, therefore, had the moat fillèd in but before the bulk of the water could be drained off into a stream above Maidens Fall, which goes into Rutters Hollow, the cellars were completely flooded by a vigorous spring which had fed the moat and water poured into the kitchens and main hall and a diver had to be employed to retrieve the contents of Old Pel's wine-cellars. While the moat had been spring-fed, the *house* was now spring-fed and the cost of pumping machinery to keep the water in the cellars at a reasonable level was about five times that of filling up the moat.

The front doors of Ineyne Manor, with the scrolled and broken pediment enclosing what successive Prunes have called "a diverted trollop" but which is, in fact, an inverted scallop, are impressive. As we waited after Percy had rung the bell, by means of a hefty, late eighteenth century lavatory chain, set to one side of the doorway, we could hear the faint clamour coming from the rear of the house and then, also coming from the rear of the house, the unsteady approach of Old Clotte with his slow tread, his occasional tripping over rugs and his crashing on to the floor boards. After glaring at us with insensate fury through the partly-opened door, the butler grudgingly let us in.

Directly in the visitor's line of sight, as he quickly turns his head on entering, to avoid old Clotte's foetid breath, is the grand staircase. This is flanked by two exquisitely carved pedestals surmounted by heraldic unicorns which hold great shields displaying armorial bearings. These 'coats of arms' are not, however, those of the Prune family but were borne by the Catholic gentleman whose manor King Henry the Eighth allowed Sir Plumstede Prune to plunder.

The staircase is fitted up with a hefty block and tackle and a bo'sun's chair. This was installed by Major Pritchard Prune on his return from the Napoleonic Wars to enable his ex-batman-valet, Trooper Stupore, to haul him up to the first floor when, after staying too long over his post-prandial port, he was incapable of climbing the stairs. He could always get down again, falling most of the way, and then, indulgent master that he was, he would hoist up Stupore. His manservant would then come down, in much the same fashion as his master, and haul the major up. This charming old tradition of yesteryear, a nightly observance which sometimes went on all night and until one or the other of the participants fell in his tracks to sleep where he fell, ceased abruptly when Stupore fell out of the chair-harness one night and broke his neck. Having nobody to haul him up to bed, the major stayed longer and ever longer over his post-prandial port so that in time his post-prandial port of one evening became the pre-prandial port of the next and his heirs finally had him committed to a Home for Incurable Drunks.*

As we stood in that old hall, a vast chamber which has seen so much history, we felt that time was meaningless, not that time appeared to stand still — just that it was meaningless. This was because of the four hundred and fifty Spanish and French clocks there — all chiming, ticking, tinkling, clanking, dinging, donging, and pealing at different speeds and showing different times. These are the 'collection' made by Major Pritchard who, with his unit following always just in the van of the main British Army throughout the Peninsular and European campaigns, had 'liberated' from houses in those districts over which the Allies had advanced. The cellars of Prune's mansion were restocked by him in the same way.** On the left of the hall is a vast fireplace and on a big Turkish rug, which Peter 'Ropey' Prune got from the Royal Air

---

* And, considering the heavy drinking traditions of his class and times, this was no mean feat.

** And emptied by him in a very short time after his return home.

Force Club (on the pretext that he knew where he could get it cleaned cheaply), is a huge, realistically-stuffed Bengal tiger. This is the same animal which ate the younger brother of Phillip in 1884 while he was the guest of the Maharaja of Marzbarre and fell off his elephant on top of the beast. A most startling example of the taxidermist's art is seen in the ankle and elastic-sided booted foot which protrudes from the right side of the tiger's jaws.

In the centre of the hall is a large Elizabethan globe of the world set on an intricately-wrought stand. This was once the property of Sir Walter Raleigh and came from his house and into the possession of Sir Pritchard Proon after Sir Walter had been imprisoned in the Tower. A great admirer of the famous explorer, Sir Pritchard petitioned the Queen to allow Lady Raleigh and Sir Walter's son to join Raleigh in the Tower, for company and comfort, and as soon as this was allowed, and the Raleigh home was quite untenanted, Sir Pritchard got the globe.

In a small glass case on the right hand wall is the embroidered cod-piece of Sir Plumstede, set alongside Sir Pritchard's decorated arras. The dominating feature of this wall, however, is that which was introduced into the manor by 'Beau' Prune during the eighteenth century when there was a universal fad for all things Chinese. It depicts a great tribe of monkeys cavorting in the most abandoned fashion and oddest contortions in a massive old brass bas-relief from Old Cathay.* Clotte, self appointed guide of visitors to Ineyne, never hesitates to point out (especially to lady visitors,) a droll flaw in this huge curio which, strangely enough, affects only the male monkeys and he will go on to explain that this occurred some ninety-seven years ago when, while stored in an outhouse, the huge brass frieze froze during the Great Frost of '77.

In turn we visited the Ante-Room, the Chintz Room, the Green Room, the North Room, the Great Room and the Bath Room. The room next to the bath-room we visited several times because of the odd effect which Bert Ullidge's cloudy beer was having on us.

*Not 'Old Cathy', as Clotte has it, *she* was a massive old brass and bar-relief at the Mug and Finger in the 'Beau's' time.

The Great Room is actually the master bedroom and contains a valuable collection of Louis XVth furniture, hangings, paintings and objets d'art. These treasures came from Chateau Praline de Prangue, Inseine-et-Silley, the seat of Comte du Praline who was nicknamed 'Poisson d'Avril' by Queen Marie Antoinette, not merely because he was a fool and born in April but also because he closely resembled a beached carp. This melancholy aristo prevailed upon his English kinsman, Patrick Prune, uncle and guardian of Pritchard, to receive the more valuable pieces from his home when it was menaced by "revolting peasants". Patrick generously undertook to house not only these valuables but also a string of blood horses which were spirited away from the Chateau to the coast and over the Channel to Sussex.

The Comte eventually escaped the guillotine and was released from prison, in return for revealing the hiding places of several of his noble friends, but not before the rough Revolutionaries had converted him into a 'sans cullottes' — not that he embraced their cause — they simply took off his trousers and turned him loose in Paris. When the Comte turned up at Prune Parva to claim his property, Patrick Prune had sold the pedigree horses and stoutly denied all knowledge of the rest of the stuff. The guide book of Ineyne Manor contains the line "Due to a tragedy of the French Revolution, this collection passed into the hands of the English branch of the family".

The Comte didn't leave matters there, however, he took up residence in a pig-sty near the back of the house and, having procured a flintlock gun, he shot lead balls at Patrick every time that gentleman ventured outside or appeared at any of the windows — the loss of his possessions had unhinged the Frenchman's brain. The Comte died of swine fever in 1817.

It was Major Pritchard who, as Lieutenant Prune, on coming of age in 1799, occupied this master bedroom and the Louis XV bed and, being on the lanky side, he found the bed uncomfortably short. Somewhat testily, because he had a terrible hangover, he asked his batman, Stupore, to get him a bigger bed.   Trooper Stupore reminded his master that it was a valuable Louis XV bed. "Well", said the young officer, "it's too short, I want a bigger one — haven't we got a XVI or, better still, a XVII?"

In slavish imitation of royalty, the Prunes have their own Waterloo Chamber but, unlike the great room at Windsor Castle, their's is not a room at all — but a chamber. It was the one which Trooper Stupore carted about on his bat-horse for the Major's use throughout his campaigns under Wellington. A huge vessel, made in Stafford, it is decorated all over with grog-blossoms and bears the inscription "Water (l'eau) Chamber". It is still to be seen under the Louis XV bed in the Great Room.

The Bath Room — which is not *the* bath room but a chamber, with eighteenth century decor and furnishings, was named after the city spa where Pel' and his son 'Beau' spent so much of their time and fortune. Here there are more objets and bric-a-brac from Chateau Praline, including an exquisite three-foot long ivory and ormolu douche, a present to the melancholy Praline from the Dauphin of France, a young prince who was so unhealthily and morbidly obsessed with his constipation.

In a massive glass case containing relics of the Battle of Waterloo, brought home by the redoubtable Major Pritchard ('Stewed') Prune, we saw a large gold-hilted, gold scabbarded sabre* which was originally carried by a colonel in Napoleon's Dragoons and formally received by Major Prune after the French defeat at Waterloo. The latter did not receive it as the traditional gesture of an enemy's surrender, he got it by holding a large, cocked and primed horse-pistol to the colonel's left temple. In the same case there is the Frenchman's silver and gold crested helmet, his silver-gilt spurs, a pair of gold buckled braces, gold collar studs, diamond studded gold watch, gold wedding ring, a miniature of his family, a silver brandy flask, (emptied within seconds of its 'presentation') a wig of black hair, the colonel's false, porcelain eye, his gold teeth and wooden leg, the original of which he'd left on the field of Fuentes D'Onoro. As we looked over these effects and reflected on their very intimate nature, we found ourselves vaguely surprised not to see the French colonel himself there.

* Clotte always has trouble with this and calls it a "gilt-holdered gold scarab."

'Prinny's' watch is also displayed in the Bath Room. Originally the property of George, Prince of Wales, it came into the major's possession after he'd gallantly offered to look after the Prince's clothes and things while 'Prinny' took a dip in the sea at Brighthelmstone.

It was in this same Bath Room that Old Pel' and young Beau Prune gathered the wits of their day, since they had so much trouble gathering their own. Most of the great wits were hard up but had a well-developed nose for hospitality and were accomplished free-loaders and since Old Pel' kept a sumptuous table and an excellent cellar, (before the moat spring flooded it) father and son had no difficulty getting guests. There, in an atmosphere of fine wine, fine linen, good food and candlelight, the table talk was brilliant and went on for hours while Pel' and his son took dinner in their rooms because the conversation was utterly incomprehensible to them both.

In another showcase the diary of Captain Percy Prune is seen opened at the first page. This relic of the gallant follower of Marlborough brings to the visitor an evocative glimpse of life long ago and also instances the penetrating powers of observation of this ancestor of Percy's. The entry (the only one in the book) is seen under the date "1st January, 1729" and it runs "Got this dairy for Crissmuss. Had eggs for breckfirst".

Set beyond the tapis vert at the rear of the house is a large cupola which, Percy told us, was designed by "Inugo Jones". When I said didn't he mean Inigo Jones he appeared surprised and said "No, Sid Jones" and went on to explain that whenever he finished a building this architect would rub his hands with glee and say "In you go Jones" and that's how he got his nickname.

Like all 18th century landowners, Old Pel' Prune loved building follies on his estate. His follies were not merely useless but picturesque landscape features, they were ill-conceived and very dangerous erections or excavations. After he had built the East Wing, which was, in later times, blown up accidentally by Phillip Prune, a good deal of it subsided when he had a 'grotto' dug out underneath it. Two Parvanians were trapped here. Two other villagers were crushed by falling masonry in his

'ruined abbey' and another three were drowned in his 'ornamental sunken Japanese Garden' when the moat was yet undrained and water broke through to fill up the excavation. Such follies were not always the result of some selfish whim on the part of eighteenth century country gentlemen — quite often they were a subtle means of giving employment to poor men of the district in hard times but when Pel' claimed this as his motive at the last of a succession of inquests, the Parva men said in effect "Don't bother — we'd rather be poor men of the district going through hard times than be crushed or drowned". The 'sunken Japanese Garden' is now called Pelham's Pool — the bodies were never recovered.

The eighteenth century saw the first ha-ha. This was a wide trench dug at the rear of a country residence, with sides steep enough to discourage cattle from approaching too near to the house. Since this made a fence unneccessary, the vista from the mansion was thus unspoiled. Pel's ha-ha, however, was a very deep canyon with precipitous sides and it had about nine feet of viscous water at the bottom. It is said that Walpole gave the ha-ha its droll name. He said that a casual stroller, coming upon the sudden declivity in the turf, would exclaim "Ha-ha!" Walpole, as a guest of Pelham Prune, was not, however, a casual stroller when he came suddenly upon his host's yawning dyke. He was trying to stay on a horse which Prune had lent him. This insane beast was bolting out of control, back to the stables. It managed to jump over the chasm and land untidily on the other side but Walpole fell off. And he didn't say "Ha-ha!" When he met his host he was a very frightened man and said "Why don't you fill in that . . . . . mantrap?" Ever since that time the Prune ha-ha has been called "Walpole's . . . . . Mantrap".

Like all great old houses, Ineyne is haunted. The trouserless spectre of the fish-faced Comte, lurks a'nights in the area where his pig-sty once stood. The spirit of Sir Plumstede Proon who lived in the reign (and in constant fear) of Henry the Eight, is quite often seen plodding down a long upstairs corridor known as 'Plumstede's Amble' — this description of the passage is apt since legend has it that Plumstede was short-sighted and he once mistook the name-plate on a bed-chamber door at Windsor for an invitation. He took it for "Amble In" and he did. A moment later he was hurled out of the room by an irate King Henry who had been cosily closeted with Anne Boleyn.

'Plumstede's Amble' is flanked on the outside wall side by a great set of mullioned windows which Clotte, as guide to visitors, refers to as 'Mulligan's Winders'. The phantom of Sir Plumstede presents an eerie sight as he ambles through the moonbeams and shadows. He comes from the Chintz Room to go through the North Room, the Great Room and the Blue Room, to the lavatory — although the quickest way is via the Blenheim Room. Sir P's navigation, as a ghost, is as inept as it was in his life at court. Apart from the 'Amble In' episode, he got a frightful duffing up when he climbed into the bed of the formidably virginal Princess ('Bloody') Mary and an even more severe going-over when he got into a bed occupied by Queen Catherine Howard *and* the king!

The family and domestics are never much dismayed at the sight of this amiable, distrait, roly-poly little Tudor Prune and will point out for him the quickest way to the 'ordinary'. Sir Plumstede, smiling a nervous thanks, will go through the nearest wall — not because that is the traditional way of ghosts but because, as a past Prune, he is a very dim phantom. When the spectre of Sir P walks the corridors of Ineyne a hideous gurgling then a high pitched weird, keening wail is heard. Strangers will blanch and take apprehensive glances over their shoulders but those in the know will say, at this noisy flushing of that ancient cistern, "Plumstede made it!"

The county newspapers were full of a discovery made at the Manor in 1953 during renovations to the kitchen area. The skeleton of a man was found in a cavity behind a wall. This grim relic would seem to evidence some tragedy of the long ago but in fact the 'bricked up' remains were those of Patrick Prune who, in 1797, got bored with hanging about the house — he couldn't go outside because of the Comte shooting at him, and so he set about some 'do it yourself' tasks. He decided to sweep all the chimneys, starting with the wide one in the main hall. Once up in the ancient sooty labyrinth he soon lost himself and the domestics heard him calling for help in the oddest parts of the house — after a week the cries ceased, and he was never heard or seen again. He'd apparently dropped into a shaft which had only one outlet — that one through which he had fallen to fetch up behind the wall from which it was impossible to hear his cries for help. Some scraps of clothing and a few pathetic artifacts, shoe buckles and buttons, established the skeleton as that of an 18th century man, but for a long time it couldn't be explained why (a) he'd been 'bricked up' and (b) why he was upside down.

Clotte, Prunes' principal retainer, who has systematically robbed the family for decades, was appointed custodian of the great house during the master's absences to act as guide whenever a certain enterprising tourist agency, called Gullible Travellers, brings bemused and travel-sick consignments of Americans across the fields and down the cart tracks to the Parva on 'Stately Homes' visits to the Manor.

Clotte's piece de resistance is the "haunted piano" in the Regency Room. This chamber is approached by 'Plumstede's Amble'. This gloomy corridor prepares the visitors for a sight of the 'haunted piano', a large grand in golden satin wood which has never been played by any member of the family since the Prunes acquired it in the early nineteenth century, although one of the chamber maids was able to pick out, with one finger, 'The Hebrew Maiden and her Christian Lover' and 'Oh Pilot 'tis a Fearful Night' back in 1904. At times during the day and night this instrument, according to Clotte, "plays itself" but in fact it just twangs, plings and plunks in an idiot sort of way. We discovered why when we lifted the lid. For something like 160 years the piano has been a sort of super council flats for a horde of mice. The twanging goes down well with the visitors and Clotte usually gets a good tip as a result. He also makes a fair income on the side by flogging such small pieces as pistols, swords, knives, forks, spoons and other crested table-ware along with the odd Prune miniature — and any miniature depicting a past Prune is distinctly odd.

The first party of American visitors to arrive at Ineyne Manor came by accident. A coach-load of them were driven up to the house back in 1951 as the result of a 'Mystery Tour' which was so shrouded in secrecy by the directors of Gullible Travellers that even the driver didn't know where he was going. He went off the main Chichester road on to a secondary road and, with a suitable show of knowing precisely where he was headed, he then struck a cart track and got deeper and deeper into the Downs. He was just about to chuck it in and confess that he was completely lost, when he fetched up at Prune Parva. When he pulled up at the Manor, with admirable sang froid, he affected to have been following a set route all the time.

Despite the grandeur of Ineyne Manor, unlike some stately residences, it has a distinct atmosphere of being lived in, not only by humans but by cats, dogs, mice, rats, cockroaches, crickets and all sorts of other things which go bump, scrape and patter during the day as well as in the night.*

Before we again risked our lives, by accepting Percy's offer of a lift from the manor to where we'd parked our trainer aircraft, he showed us his study. Most of the floor of this room is occupied by his mother's relief map of Sussex. It is not, however, a relief map in the accepted sense — one of those in bas relief — showing high and low ground in papier mache or plaster of Paris, but a huge, overblown affair showing every ladies' 'leau', lav', twinkle-house and whatsit in the county. Lady Priscilla had it made for herself after a most distressing tour of East and West Sussex on a series of charity drives so that whenever she set out on a drive to raise funds and sit on committees she could list the exact places where she *could* sit — between committees and things.

Percy gave us a privileged look at a great tome in which the Prune family records are kept — known as 'Ye Logge Booke'. The Master of Ineyne told me that he is using it to write up the history of his family from that Roman ancestor, Persius Prunus, (AD 92 - AD 141) who,

* These of course include the famous bats in the Prune Belfry.

by knocking over the lamp in his family's home-shrine, caused the great fire of Rome, to his grandfather, Phillip Prune (1860 - 1903) a noted speed-fiend and road hog in his times, who died at the age of forty-three years and at a speed of thirty-five mph, together with three friends to whom he was giving a lift. Percy told me that he may write the whole book "under a psodynymph". Since, as it was once expressed, "such a high standard of fatuously exuberant bone-headedness could not have been achieved in Prune's life alone — that heredity must have played a part —" that "generations of Prune undoubtedly lived, boobed and died before the sum total of their cosmic ineptitude could be concentrated in one human frame", the present author believes that his publisher may commission him at some future date to work with Percy, at Ineyne, to produce the entire history of this celebrated family.

With this thought in mind we quit Ineyne Manor.

SQUIRE PERCY TODAY

To say that Percy is luckier than most of us who lived through his period of history is to understate. Percy, having cut his own wide swathe of destruction during his six years of war-time flying, emerged unscathed, whereas there must still be ex-airman trying for some addition to their pensions because they just happened to be around when Percy had a hand in 'their' war. He manages to live on quite well at the family home in spite of his continued ineptitude. He even ventured into the poultry business but made an error or two in his orders so that he finished up with four thousand fierce cock birds in the acres around Ineyne and these fought each other, indulged in cannabalism, cornered 'Groupy', the bull-terrier, in Fairy's Bottom and almost pecked him to death and then laid siege to the manor itself so that Percy had to organise a shoot. Through a contact at the Stock Exchange he got gangs of young stockbrokers to come and shoot the arrogant, rampant Rhode Island Reds, giving them all they could bag. Everybody at Ineyne and in fact everybody in the Parva had to practically live on

chicken for months before all traces of his poultry venture
had gone.

Prune's name appears in a well-known reference book about well-known people and here he has it that his recreations are 'Motoring, cycling and walking'. The first of these he indulges in to the peril and terror of everyone else on the highway. The other two recreations he indulges in to his own peril whenever his Lagonda and also his mother's 1925 Rolls Royce are in dock for repairs after accidents, or during those periods when his licence has been taken away from him by the authorities.

He is as well known in the casualty wards of Sussex hospitals as any visiting surgeon — almost as well known as he is in the police courts of the county. Those who knew Prune in war-time will recall that he had a mascot, an irascible wire-haired fox-terrier called 'Binder'. The dog was demobbed, after hostilities, with his master and lived on to a ripe old age at Ineyne — his pedigree has it that he was sired by 'Intruder out of Bandit'.

'Binder's' last resting place is at the back of the manor. Lady Priscilla had a soft spot for the choleric, testy terrier who, for his part, found several she didn't know she had — having bitten her frequently — even so, she regularly tends his grave, having planted it with dog daisies and dog roses.

Nowadays Percy keeps an overweight, bibulous bull-terrier called 'Groupy', once the drinking companion of a real 'Groupy' — one, Group Captain 'Grog' Blossumme, whose ultimate passing was accompanied by the most frightful delerium tremens. The dog was foisted on to Percy by the executor of 'Grog's' estate in the bar of the Mug and Finger Inn. 'Groupy' has a marked penchant for strong drink — his favourite tipple being barley wine. Each morning the bull-terrier tools off down the lane to the Mug and Finger at a time when he knows that Bert Ullidge will be bottling up his shelves for the day's trading and he takes advantage of Bert's frequent absences from the bar, as the Guv'nor totes out the empties to the yard, to not merely lap up the 'swipes', that beer which has spilled into trays under the taps, but also takes bottles of barley wine from the lower shelves, whips off the caps with his tough jaws, spills the liquor on the floor and laps it up in time to be on the public's side of the bar, with a silly grin on his face, by the time Bert returns. By opening time he is usually half sloshed.

Because Percy has several times been sued by the 'stately homes' visitors when 'Groupy' has gone for them, he getting pot-valiant and agressive in his cups, he has to be lured, by means of a dish of brandy, into the cellars during the time parties are being shown over the place. Here, in Old Pel' Prune's cellars, he indulges in much the same sort of 'drink-in' as those in which eighteenth century gents, like Sir Francis Dashwood of the Hell Fire Club, went in for and once he was forgotten and stayed down there for forty-eight hours. He was finally discovered, spark out, surrounded by two dozen bottles, some of which had contained cherry brandy and two of Chateau Praline de Prangue champagne. That he was quite insensible was as well because several inches of twisted champagne wire and a shard or two of cherry brandy bottle glass was firmly embedded in his chops.

Percy rushed him off to a vet' in Chichester where he was to be kept for a drying out period but, after twenty-four hours on an egg and milk diet, he escaped and got back to Ineyne in seven days. He could have made it in three but there were too many pubs on the way.

Prune occasionally surfaces from the depths of the country to attend reunions. He is an enthusiastic attender of reunions, so enthusiastic in fact that he attends reunions of units to which he was never attached, those of squadrons with which he never flew, of services he had never joined and commands which wouldn't have had him if you'd paid them but since people *do* change in appearance over the years he's not often discovered and can put up some convincing, if outrageous, 'lines' about his war-time exploits.

His social life in London is largely taken care of in this counterfeit fashion but while he attends so many reunions where he is not known, he has never attended two reunions where he would be known — those of his old Prangmere squadron and one arranged by a kinsman of his in Paris. There is a sound reason for his never getting to the Prangmere do's. The Hon' Sec', an efficient gent' called Clarke, who was indeed a clerk on the squadron and is, inevitably, known as 'Nobby', had several war-time brushes with Percy and always sends Percy's invitation to a wrong address — intentionally, thus, when it is returned "Not Known", in a twisted 'Orderly Room' sort of way, honour is satisfied with a "Well, we *did* ask him!"

Prune's opposite number in what has been called, with honour, 'The Fighting French Air Force' which is, or rather was, more formally, the Free French Air Force, was a certain Aspirant Praline.

Pierre Praline, who is tenuous kin to Prune — on the French side of the family, is apparently a glutton for punishment — still fired with that wonderful spirit which used to be known, 'way back', as the Entente Cordial. Pierre Praline's own story, his war-time exploits and 'civvy street' (— or could it, in his case, be 'rue civil?) vicissitudes, must be recounted at another time — they compare favourably, if that's the word, with Prune's. Thus, 'like calling to like', P.P. has asked P.P. to Paris for a "Fighters Pilots" get-together every year. Percy has never quite made it. For one who cannot find his way to a rendezvous in his own capital city, it is perhaps asking a lot to expect him to get to one in another country. Praline is a shade more alert than Percy and is always on time in the right place but although he hasn't changed *that* much in appearance, Percy always manages to miss him although he always counts his visits to Paris a success, having formed an interesting association with a certain Mam'selle Suzette Ardoure whom he met some years ago on the plane going over.

On those occasions when Percy has gone to Town by train — or has had to take to a train somewhere on the way, through colliding on the road with another vehicle, he has proved a sitting bird for that now fast-disappearing race — the ex-service con' man. They still lurk at termini on the look-out for any mug of comparitive age who may be sporting a regimental or service tie. One such silver-tongued rogue, with a large handlebar moustache, spotted Percy who was wearing a

Royal Air Force tie — the con' man was wearing a (beer-spotted) Guards tie but retired to a corner of the station buffet, groped in his scuffed brief case and produced this 'own' RAF tie and, putting it on, he came up to Percy at the bar with a "My dear fellow! How great to see you looking so well after all this time!"

They were soon downing double scotches — bought by Percy. The latter, was by now convinced that he had met an old comrade but couldn't for the life of him think where they had met. He was a sucker for the next line put in at what the con' man knew to be the right moment — "Hate to bring it up, old boy, but you *will* recall that fiver I lent you in the mess — just before I was posted. Could you possibly see your way to letting me have it back?"

Percy stumped up without a murmur. It is really surprising how many of us veterans will fall for something like this — it's not surprising that Percy falls for it every time.

Prune had another encounter which cost him more money and more scotch and also resulted in his attending the wrong reunion. He had heard of his old squadron reunion through an aquaintance in Sussex and he made toward the rendezvous in Piccadilly after his run-in with the con' man who, despite the vigilance of the Railway Police, had successfully 'done' the Golden Arrow Bar at Victoria for a while. He'd got the date wrong of course and he found himself, a rare male, at the reunion of 'Class Number 38, WAAF Teleprinter Course, Cranwell, 1941.'

Within thirty minutes he was out on the street again — ejected by the management at the urging of several matrons — ex-WAAFs, to whom he had tried to tell a series of crude stories about the boudoir antics of WAAFs and pilots — dirty yarns he'd mugged up for the reunion — not this one but his old Prangmere 'do'.

Perhaps the weirdest company Prune has ever got himself into was that which gathered for an 'Old Girls' Tea' at an hotel in Knightsbridge. The WAAF affair had been organised for what the participants referred to in a jolly way as 'us old girls' but here were *really* old girls. Decades ago they had attended 'St Clothilde's Boarding

School for the Daughters of Colonial-Serving Gentlemen.'
Percy, after a lunch-time thrash at the RAF Club (of which he is not a member) breezed into the hotel lounge, well-oiled, and started in to importune an octogenarian dowager who'd been Head Girl of St Clothilde's at the outbreak of the First World War. He'd told her a couple of ripe yarns and was launching into that one about the gay guardee who joined the Commandoes when he was grabbed by two stewards. St Clothilde's ceased to be a 'Boarding School' for the Ds of C-S Gs in 1947 and became a training establishment for physical training instructresses but by courteous tradition, the Principal, a certain Miss Leslie Biane, provided the old girls with stewards in the form of some of her pupils — to fetch and carry the odd tot for the ladies, sandwiches and cake and to help them out of their chairs to visit the twinkle house. Leslie Biane got the drift of Percy's yarning and saw that the dowager's complexion was going from scarlet to puce and told off two of her hefty trainees to give him the bum's rush. The two young Amazons collared Prune and dragged him out of the room. They kneed him twice in the vestibules or it may have been that they kneed him once in both vestibules — before pushing him out into Knightsbridge.

It was on the occasion of a sort of reunion that I saw him last. I was on my way to his club on a Sunday — we were to talk over the possibility of my editing that 'Logge Booke' of his and, miraculously, he'd got time and date right. It was a bright morning in March when I saw him in a body of marching men. These were ex-Irish Guardsmen and Guardees who, every Sunday-before-St Patrick's-Day make an annual march to the Guards Memorial in civilian clothes (or do the Guards call it mufti?) bowler-hatted with umbrellas at the trail. These quandam guards wear their bowlers as they were wont to wear their bearskin and service caps, well forward. Percy affects this guardee fashion but his hat is not merely well forward but almost right over his eyes. It was this fact which had caused him to veer off the pavement at one point and inadvertently join the Guards.

I followed to see what would happen. As that smart

body of men reached a point near Number One London, Apsley House, the one-time town-house of that doyen of all Guards, Wellington, they turned in the direction of the Memorial. Percy marched straight on and into a vicious tangle of taxis and cars and an ominous bearing-down of omnibuses.

Miraculously he survived, though he created a frightful pile-up of traffic. He gained the opposite pavement, tripped but kept his pace and then descended the steps of the Ladies where he was lost to sight.

Several ladies came up rather hurriedly after he'd gone down. His case, I heard later, came up and, for all that I know now — Percy could have 'gone down'.